Love Among the Gods: Myths of Relationship

by
Shirley Kiefer

Love Among the Gods: Myths of Relationship

Preface 4

Myth as a Mirror of Inner Wholeness...5

Hera and Zeus: First Couple of Olympus 11

Isis and Osiris: Love and Regeneration in Egypt.......................24

Persephone and Hades: Love in the Underworld 31

Artemis and Apollo: Sister and Brother 38

Aphrodite and Her Lovers: Love and War and Others 46

Jason and Medea: Quest of the Golden Fleece 55

Theseus and Ariadne: Love and Abandonment 66

Perseus and Medusa: Conquest of the Gorgon 77

Psyche and Eros: Soul and Spirit..86

Epilogue 99

Acknowledgements..100

Suggested Reading and Additional Resources 101

Index 104

Preface

Mythology holds up a mirror to our inner life as humans, showing us how our personality and choices affect our lives. Myths of partnership not only impart wisdom about male-female relationships, but also about the balance of male and female qualities within us as individuals.

These stories from Greek (and one Egyptian) mythology are fascinating tales not only of love relationships, but also of the human quest for wholeness within.

Zeus and Hera are the perennial love/hate couple. Isis and Osiris bring new life out of tragedy. Jason and Medea show us what manipulation is like. Theseus and Ariadne deal with abandonment. Perseus learns to integrate his feminine side as part of his heroic quest. Psyche and Eros mature through the trials their union produced.

Shirley Kiefer retells these stories with new insight for our time. A retired librarian with a background in world religions, mythology and psychology, she helps us see their characters as parts of ourselves, giving us glimpses into these archetypal forces we all experience.

Whether you read these as literal partnership stories or as individual quests for wholeness, you will delight in rehearing these ancient tales in contemporary language.

Myth as a Mirror of Inner Wholeness

Far up on a sun drenched mountaintop, handsome talented gods and beautiful wise goddesses are seated around a table, laughing and drinking ambrosia from golden goblets. Radiant, assertive, confidant of their own power, they joke, flirt, orate and perform for one another. When tired of each other, they turn and view the antics of mortal creatures down below, which they may visit anytime over the rainbow bridge leading down to earth.

Despite my adult left-brain disparagement of this childhood fantasy as a superficial paradise, it is a persistent image that refuses to fade. Even though I am now much better acquainted with each of those deities and have experienced many of their characteristic flaws firsthand, I continue to believe that the Olympian gods and goddesses, highest expression of divinity for those ancient wise Greeks, surely had some answers to the ageless, contemporary quest for love and fulfillment. Or did they? Perhaps it depends on what kind of answers we seek and even how we ask the question.

Gods and Goddesses of old did indeed experience love in all its forms—erotic, platonic, familial, lustful, playful, painful, jealous, and exploitative—even as we humans do. Virtually every type of love that humans experience in everyday life is portrayed in the Greek myths. Ecstasy (Hera and Zeus are said to have had a honeymoon lasting 300 years), platonic companionship (the chaste Artemis and her beloved hunting companion Orion), rape (Hades and Persephone), short-term affairs (Aphrodite), philandering (Zeus), manipulation (Jason and Medea), rejection and abandonment (Theseus and Ariadne), infidelity (most of them), and occasionally a committed love (Psyche and Eros) are all there.

It is somewhat startling to discover that there are few models in mythology for marriage as we view it. Instead there are a wide variety of relationships that run the gamut of human emotions. The Olympians seem to express life as it is rather than some inhuman ideal of perfection. That may be why we are so fond of them and also why, in the end, they may have more to say to us than an inhuman ideal. For they hold up a mirror to us as we are and enable us to see ourselves with our flaws as well as our virtues. They serve in some way the same purpose as the clown in North American Indian tradition, a character who enacted an exaggeration of someone's foolishness to make that person more aware.

By holding up flaws and virtues in larger-than-life scenarios, the Olympians do give answers as to how we sabotage ourselves and others in the quest for fulfillment. They show where we go wrong, as well as right, and leave the final answers and decisions up to each one of us as to how we use that information in our own lives.

If we choose to emulate the philandering of Zeus, the sulky jealousy of Hera, the competitiveness of Artemis, the manipulation of Aphrodite, we shall reap the consequences. If we choose to grow like Psyche in her trials, to move on to higher gods like Ariadne when abandoned by Theseus, to tune into an understanding of our adversary like Perseus with

Medusa, then we can also experience the rewards. It's all up to us.

And so, with this perspective, let us look at some of these Olympians and see what they show us in their choices. Assisting us in this process today is the work of Jungian psychology, a perspective not available to the ancient Greeks, but undoubtedly in their consciousness. For the psychologist Carl Jung merely recognized and articulated the value of archetypal symbols in Greek mythology which have always been there. Numerous other therapists today are expanding his work in this area and interpreting this symbolism in ways that touch all of us in our contemporary lives.

It was after teaching and working with Jean Bolen's *Goddesses in Everywoman* that I began to realize the relevance of ancient mythology for my own life when viewed from a Jungian perspective. Inevitably the question arose as to how myths of gods and goddesses in relationship could speak to male-female relationships today? While working on this theme, another issue presented itself simultaneously to me. What do these myths of relationship have to say about the integration of masculine and feminine qualities within the individual?

Thus I began to view myths of relationship from a double perspective. First, how do myths of male and female archetypes as represented in gods and goddesses, or in mythological heroes and heroines, provide insight into men-women relationships today? Secondly, what do these myths say to us about integrating the so-called "masculine" and "feminine" polarities within ourselves for greater wholeness as individuals?

The first part of this book will deal with myths of Greek gods and goddesses in relationship. We will delve briefly into Egyptian mythology for the story of Isis and Osiris as a basis of comparison with the Greek tales. It is one of the most moving stories of love in mythology, and some of its themes are echoed in the later Greek myths. The second section will look at myths involving relationships among mortals. Since these are at the same time stories of heroic journeys or quests, they are also stories of initiation into the heroic life and provide insight into each personal journey toward individuation.

Carl Jung was among the first scholars in psychology to concern himself with the way in which ordinary people can rise to their higher potential by understanding their own inner process of emotional development. He described the process of conscious inner growth as the way of individuation, wherein the individual learns to move from unconscious reaction based on primal emotion to conscious choice of reaction based on understanding of one's whole being.

Both dreams and myths were among the tools that Jung used for self-understanding in the journey of individuation from unconscious impulse to conscious balanced behavior. Dreams provide highly personal symbols from the unconscious and when understood can give much insight into the dreamer's inner needs and sense of balance or imbalance. Often these personal symbols are universal in their association and hence become archetypal or representative of states of feeling and behavior common to people everywhere.

Mythology is another way in which archetypal symbols are expressed. Because myths arise out of ancient oral tradition in which people expressed their fears and longings, their joys and sorrows, their questions about the meaning of life events in a shared way, the characters and symbolism become collective archetypes with which we can all have common associations. As such, myths provide a rich array of archetypal behavior from which we can gain a deeper understanding of ourselves as human beings.

Many of the mythological characters illuminate in a dramatic way the psychological concepts of Jung. His concept of the anima and animus as the unexpressed qualities of the opposite sex within each individual can be more clearly understood when viewing a relationship like that of Artemis and Apollo. These opposing aspects often express themselves in inappropriate ways because we fail to understand their presence in our makeup. Jung's concept of the shadow element within each person, that part of ourselves that we sometimes label "bad" or "negative" because we do not understand its purpose and therefore often repress until it erupts explosively, can be seen more clearly in a character like Medea.

As we delve into each of the following mythological relationships, viewing them from their archetypal perspective, may our own journey of individuation be enhanced. We begin to sense the Hera or Zeus, the Jason or Medea in ourselves and become aware of its influence upon us. Only then can we begin to consciously choose our behavior to ensure the kind of balance and wholeness we most desire.

Hera and Zeus: First Couple of Olympus

When we think of relationships among the gods, the first that comes to mind is Zeus and Hera, the primary partnership relation, the King and Queen of Olympus. And indeed they are the Greek expression of the male female polarity, which exists in other mythologies as the Roman Jupiter and Juno, the Egyptian Osiris and Isis, the Norse Woden and Frigga, the Hebrew Adam and Eve, the medieval Arthur and Guinevere.

Every mythology recognizes the male-female polarity that underlies the forming of human life and expresses itself in the two sexes. Although there are some androgynous gods (Hermaphrodite) and independent goddesses (Athena), most of the Olympians function within a sexual polarity, just as humans. Even when there is a mythology of an Original Great Mother, as in Crete or as with the Celtic Danu or Hindu Kali, she combines both polarities within herself, but splits into the two sexes in succeeding generations. This is the inevitable recognition of the Chinese Yin/Yang polarity of light and dark, or the active and receptive modes of being. They are always pictured with the ideogram of two intertwining parts of a complete circle.

The Yin/Yang perspective helps us to view the basic polarity in a non-sexist way that the male-female mythologies do not. It expands the polarity into concepts of consciousness and unconsciousness, into the positive and negative energy. Both are necessary for a complete whole. As such, the

Yin/Yang description is becoming more and more popular as we struggle to overcome sexual stereotyping. At the same time, it is much harder to relate to an abstract principle than to a dramatic persona. I therefore propose that we try to combine the wisdom of the Chinese perspective and the colorful humanity of the Greek mythology to enjoy both without bogging down in sexual stereotypes of supposed masculine and feminine behavior.

For it seems to me that those mythologies beginning with a single entity that subdivides or multiplies into the two polarities come closest to the human experience. We do begin life as a single cell and subdivide into more. Before birth we are in symbiosis with the mother until we emerge into the world and begin to individuate.

In the process of individuation we discover that we possess both Yin and Yang qualities and that life is a process of understanding and balancing them. Whether we live in partnership with a person of the opposite sex or the same sex or live alone, that same balancing process takes place in all of us individually.

In a sense, there is an inner love affair going on within each of us, paralleling the outer relationships in our lives. And the quality of the inner affair may well determine the quality of the outer one. Learning to love ourselves, to appreciate and balance our own Yin/Yang qualities is no small thing. Indeed it is the first step to good relationships in the outer world.

Greek mythology gives us delightful stories of gods and goddesses, demigods of both human and divine parentage, and ordinary mortals wrestling with this balance.

In them we can clearly see where there is an imbalance and the consequences. They give us a concrete example of qualities in and out of balance which we can recognize in our own lives. As we look at the balancing act going on in several mythical relationships, I propose that we view it on two levels. At one level, they are stories of a literal male and female relationship, with all the perils and rewards of a romantic pairing. On another level, the characters can also be viewed as the Yin and Yang polarities within each one of us that we must each learn to balance within ourselves. Additional ways of viewing these inner polarities can be seen in the complementary forms below.

Yang	Yin
active	receptive
thinking	feeling
rational	intuitive
mind	emotions
conscious	unconscious
analytic	empathic
differentiated	holistic
competition	cooperation
left brain	right brain

Zeus and Hera are a good starting point. Originally brother and sister, they were the offspring of two Titans, Cronos and Rhea. The mythical Titans were the progeny of Heaven (Uranus) and Earth (Gaia), who sprang from original Chaos in the Greek creation account. Earth and Heaven produced various offspring, including monsters and the giant Titans. According to mythology, Uranus kept most of his offspring imprisoned, lest he be overpowered by them. Considering how their human descendents have since polluted earth and air, he may have been right to be concerned! However, Mother Gaia, whose instinctive urge is to procreate and nourish, was upset by this autocratic assumption of power and urged her son Cronos to take action to change the situation. The will to power is a strong force and expressed itself symbolically in Cronos' castration of his father, symbolically disempowering Uranus and seizing power for himself and his Titan siblings. This familiar motif of the young king replacing the old or the son replacing the father is found in many ancient mythologies and expresses the need for new energy to replace waning virility.

Mating with his sister Rhea (another name for the Great Mother), Cronos knew he could not trust his own offspring either, so he swallowed each one as it was born. Rhea, symbol of the feminine life force, enraged at this thwarting of life and growth by masculine power, decided to enlist one of her progeny to overcome Cronos in his turn. When Zeus was born, she hid him and presented a swaddled stone to Cronos to swallow. Zeus subsequently killed his father and freed his siblings, creating the pantheon of Olympic gods and goddesses so familiar to us. Interestingly enough, Cronos, who was responsible for beginning and ending a new succession of power, gives his name to the concept of chronological time. Cronos time or chronological time is that linear historical time marked by different generations, established by the beginning and ending of outer events.

Setting himself up as new King of the Gods, Zeus chose his beautiful sister, Hera as his Queen, thus acknowledging the importance of the male-female polarity. In actuality, though, this partnership reflected the patriarchal view of the ancient Greeks that the masculine principle of power and strategy, or rational thinking, was the more important. Certainly Zeus felt no sense of commitment to his feminine partner Hera. Although he loved her and honored her publicly as his official queen, he greatly enjoyed pursuing power and pleasure elsewhere, frequently abandoning her for love affairs with other goddesses and beautiful women among the newer race of humans, leaving a trail of demigods begotten on human lovers. Hercules and Perseus were among the latter. Helen of Sparta, whose abduction by Paris of Troy caused the Trojan War, was his daughter by a mortal woman. Apollo and Artemis, Hermes, the nine Muses; and some say Dionysius were among offspring from affairs with other Titans. Persephone he fathered on his sister Demeter. Numerous other characters in mythology are said to be fathered by Zeus. It is somewhat telling that his major offspring with his Queen Hera was Ares, the God of Battle. Obviously all was not well between Zeus and Hera if they mainly produced War! Their relationship was always more or less a battle between the two over his infidelity.

They also had a daughter named Eris, meaning Discord. It was Discord who set in action a train of events that culminated in the Trojan War. Angered at being uninvited to a wedding reception on Olympus, Discord appeared anyway, bearing a golden apple. Cannily inscribing it as a prize for the fairest goddess, Discord knew it would set Hera, Athena and Aphrodite in competition with each other for the prize. It was the resolution of this competition that eventually triggered the Trojan War, according to mythology.

Zeus seems to represent the masculine principle when it is not fully united with the feminine, thus producing War or Discord. There is no real understanding or integrating of the Yang qualities with the Yin. His is the reckless promiscuity of the masculine expression without regard for the consequences on his chosen lovers brought about by the wrath of the jealous Hera, whose feelings he ignored. Most of his hapless lovers suffered Hera's punishment, regardless of their innocence. Often the offspring did as well. Hera sent two serpents to destroy Hercules as an infant, but he proved his great strength by strangling them instead, even though an infant.

In his role as king, Zeus was equally capricious. Although wise in a crafty way and quite good at lying and deception, especially to his feminine side, his wisdom lacked the compassion and justice of his parthenogenetic daughter Athena, whom he conceived by the Titan Metis (Wisdom). Warned by Gaia that progeny by Metis would be more powerful than he, Zeus swallowed Metis and the unborn

Athena, who later sprang full grown from his forehead. Undoubtedly the labor must have given him a headache, just as women's wisdom today often gives a headache to the man intent on retaining his own control of things. Feminists today see this story as a patriarchal attempt to absorb feminine wisdom and credit it to the masculine polarity, thus removing it from the feminine sphere where it is expressed in a nurturing rather than authoritative way.

However we choose to view the birth of Athena, she does represent a higher justice than Zeus, who was noted more for favoritism and scheming to maintain power than for fair judgments. For instance, he refused to make a decision about which goddess should be awarded the golden apple brought by Discord, not wanting to anger Hera, Athena or Aphrodite. Zeus craftily put the burden on Paris of Troy. Paris, as we all know, decided on the basis of bribery and chose Aphrodite when she promised him Helen of Sparta, the most beautiful woman alive. Unfortunately Helen was already married to a Greek king. It was her abduction by Paris, son of the king of Troy, which started the famous Trojan War between Troy and the Greeks.

To avenge this prominent theft, the Greeks amassed a mighty fleet under the leadership of Helen's husband, King Menelaus of Sparta, and laid siege to Troy. They succeeded in recovering Helen after employing the ruse of giving as a gift a mammoth wooden horse with soldiers hidden inside. The famous Trojan Horse gained them entry into the city of Troy and victory in the war.

Instead of supporting his victim Paris and the cause of Troy, which he secretly favored, Zeus abandoned them at the insistence of Hera, with whom he was already in trouble. Shrewdness he possessed, but not integrity.

Many classical scholars interpret the domestic conflict between Zeus and Hera as a mythological interpretation of the cultural conflict caused by the ascendancy of patriarchy in the ancient world, imposing a different social system on the earlier matriarchal societies such as Crete, where the primary worship was that of the Great Earth Mother or the White Goddess, as Robert Graves calls her. Whether or not there was a true matriarchy in ancient times, there were fertility cults based on goddess worship, with possibly matrilinear rulership.

From the standpoint of anthropology, this seems plausible. It is certainly one level of interpretation, which I see as an accurate one. I believe we can go deeper than the anthropological level, however, and look at the conflict as the emerging ego consciousness, which we associate with the Yang polarity or masculine principle (Zeus) differentiating itself from the primordial Chaos or from the all powerful Mother Goddess (Gaia, Rhea) in whom the Yin polarity or primitive feminine principle of pure life-nurturing force threatens the individual ego seeking to develop its own power. We see in Zeus a primitive form of the ego, lustily and zestfully expressing its new-found authority. Aware only of its conscious needs, it is not really in touch with its shadow side, the Yin polarity of hidden emotion, the unconscious side, the unified consciousness that sees life holistically.

Certainly Hera is a primitive expression of the Yin polarity in her turn. Daughter of Rhea and granddaughter of Gaia, earth mothers too close to nature to be distinguished from its raw, primitive threatening aspect, she is a threat to the conscious ego. This all-encompassing feminine force is ultimately dealt with in patriarchal mythology, as in civilization, by downgrading it to a beauty queen given to emotional outbursts, not to be taken seriously by the emerging ego. She is to be abandoned when she threatens the authority of the ego or to be cajoled and wooed when her softer qualities are desired.

Hera could be a beneficent force, as when she assisted Jason or her other favorites, but she is mostly portrayed as venting her jealous wrath on Zeus' mistresses. The unfortunate Io, turned into a heifer by Zeus to save her from Hera's wrath, was continually hounded by a gnat fly sent by Hera. Leta, mother of Apollo and Artemis, was punished with severe labor pains by Hera when giving birth to the twins. Hera is raw emotion not yet balanced by the mature mind, the masculine polarity. There is one myth that she conceived Hephaestus, god of fire and the smith, on her own, without a father, to show that she could reproduce without Zeus just as he had produced Athena alone. Hephaestus was born lame, symbolizing his incompleteness. Furious at this betrayal of her competence, Hera thrust him from Olympus in disgust. It is interesting to note that the lame Hephaestus is the god whom Aphrodite, goddess of love and beauty, chose to marry. My private theory is that she knew he would not be able to keep up with her other amours and was therefore easier to cuckold!

Actually the association is probably the fiery aspect of love or the connection between craftsmen and inspiration.

Greek mythology had trouble portraying a marriage in balance, achieving their famous Golden Mean. The competent goddesses were ones who functioned on their own. Athena and Artemis were the so-called virgin goddesses, sufficient unto themselves and never married. Demeter, goddess of harvest and grain, had a daughter, but did not marry. It was the maternal relationship that characterized her. Aphrodite married Hephaestus, but had numerous other lovers. Hera was the only goddess who championed marriage and committed partnership, yet her male partner did not. Just as Zeus may well be a composite of various near eastern gods in an effort to champion a masculine deity appropriate to a rising patriarchy, so Hera can perhaps be viewed as a downgrading of the omnipotent Mother Goddess concept of the ancient world as it moved away from a matriarchal or matrilinear system. Again, this is an anthropological explanation.

On a deeper level, the partnership of Zeus and Hera could represent the Yang ego seeking to establish itself and function on its own, with only a vague understanding of the need for integration with the unconscious Yin element. There is a willingness to connect with it when that is useful, but no real integration because the ego is still seeking to define itself and needing to emphasize control.

We live in an age when the assertion of ego and a sense of control is the guiding principle in our politics, economy, industry and science. Zeus still reigns with only an occasional nod to Hera when it suits his purpose. Intuitive hunches are valued in the business world if they make money; otherwise they may well be laughed at. The bottom line is profit and control.

Fortunately, psychology is helping us to see what happens on a personal level when we are preoccupied with Zeus and ignore Hera. Unacknowledged emotions do not go meekly away, any more than Hera meekly accepted her lack of acknowledgment by Zeus. They fester and often erupt into the conscious world with a vehemence or violence that catches us by surprise. Just as a smoldering volcano eventually roars into action so mass murder, assassinations, and other violence breaks out in our communities. Alternatively, these emotions may also turn inward into depression and lack of vitality, sometimes manifesting in illness or paralysis of will. The popularity of tranquilizers and anti-depressant drugs, not to mention illegal drugs, attests to this problem in society.

Jung's work in helping individuals to tap into the Yin side, to get in touch with these inner feelings often unknown to the conscious analytical mind and to tap into the intuitive wisdom of the right brain, frequently unacknowledged by the rational, linear left brain, is an important part of restoring Hera to full partnership with Zeus. As we learn to tune into the wisdom of our dreams and open up receptively to the intuitive, imaginative process of the right brain, we bring ourselves into a more healthy Yang/Yin balance. Education today is recognizing the need to develop right brain capabilities of imagination and creativity.

We are at a point where both personally and globally we need to honor and acknowledge Hera- Rhea - Gaia in a deeper way. We need to listen receptively in the Yin way to our deepest feelings and yearnings. Only in that way can we learn to be sensitive also to the inner rhythms of the natural world, respecting and working with them rather than seeking to exert control over them. The Yin approach is the holistic one that is concerned with the welfare of the entire person (mind, body and emotions) as well as the health of the whole planet. Nationalistic ego strivings and industrial megacomplexes must become aware of the needs of the downtrodden parts of the planet, whether they be human, plant or animal. Then we need to join that sensitivity and empathy to the rational mind that can consciously choose solutions from the intuitive and put them into action on the conscious level.

Hera standing alone can wallow in her emotions and inner grievances and erupt into vengeful, sometimes violent action. Together, when Hera is acknowledged and supported by Zeus, they can bring about a balance of mind and feeling, rationality and imagination, control and relaxation, left brain and right brain unity that honors the whole person.

Whole persons in turn are sensitive to the needs of the whole universe rather than isolated in their own ego struggle for control. Personal healing and global health are both enhanced when Zeus and Hera are in true balance. It is said that their original honeymoon lasted 300 years before their conflicts began. Zeus has had plenty of time since to indulge his ego and to know its limitations. Hera has had a lot of time to rage and express disappointment. It is time for a second honeymoon based on realistic understanding of one another and a new willingness to communicate and work things out, for the sake of the future of humanity and the planet.

Isis and Osiris: Love and Regeneration in Egypt

Departing from Greek mythology for a moment, it is worthwhile to look at the Egyptian counterpart of the first couple, Isis and Osiris. The Egyptians developed their mythology long before the Greeks. Isis as the feminine principle was far more important than Hera. This may be because Isis is closer to the matrilinear period of history in the ancient world. She was already referred to as the "Great Isis" in the Pyramid Texts about 3000 B.C. She has been described as the "most complete flowering of the Goddess concept in human history." Her counterparts in the ancient world were the Sumerian Inanna with her seasonally dying lover Dumuzi, the later Assyro-Babylonian Ishtar paired with her annual lover Tammuz, and the Phoenician Astarte linked with Adonis. In the Greek pantheon she is really the unified original of Aphrodite, Hera, Demeter and Persephone, for she is lover, wife and mother, all in one, as well as Queen of the Underworld.

In the Egyptian story of creation, the Sky (Nut) separated from the Earth (Geb) and from them came two sons, Osiris who ruled the fertile fields, and Set who ruled the desert, and two daughters, Isis and Nephthys. Isis and Osiris fell in love and married, so Set paired with Nephthys. Osiris, with his beautiful wife Isis, goddess of love and beauty, ruled wisely and well his territory, leading to prosperity for the people, and was greatly loved by all. Their great love and popularity made Set deeply jealous, for he too desired Isis and wanted the love and respect Osiris enjoyed as her husband. Set therefore intrigued to find a way to get rid of Osiris, that he might take his place. Summoning honored guests to a banquet, Set brought forth a wooden sarcophagus tailored to the exact measurements of Osiris and decreed that the winner of the entertainment would be he who best fit in the box. No one did, of course, except Osiris. When he lay down in it, Set jumped forward, nailed the lid fast and hauled it off to the Nile, where it was rudely shoved into the water.

  When Isis heard what had happened to her beloved Osiris, she wept and determined that she would seek his body for a proper burial. Grieving, she searched from one end of the Nile to the other, hoping his coffin may have floated to shore. Eventually she heard that a magnificent cedar pillar had been found and built into a room of the palace in neighboring Byblos in Phoenicia. Disguising herself as an old woman she came to the palace searching for the pillar which she suspected was Osiris' coffin. Attracted by a sweet odor she discovered the cedar pillar and was sure it was Osiris.

  In a story from which the Greeks later borrowed in their tale of Demeter grieving for her daughter Persephone, Isis became the nursemaid of the royal baby to be near Osiris. Planning to give the royal child immortality by holding him in the fire at night, she was discovered by the child's mother. Whereupon she revealed her true identity as Isis and claimed the pillar of Osiris. Her wish granted the grieving widow took it on a boat back to Egypt, where she opened it and made love with the dead Osiris. Love was able to bring life out of death and she conceived a son Horus.

Set in his rage had the body of Osiris hacked to pieces and strewn in the marshes of the Nile. Once again the grieving Isis set out in a boat to gather together the pieces of Osiris. She managed to find all of them except for his phallus, which was now part of the river, giving the Nile the power of bringing fertility upon the land. Thereafter Isis, Osiris and Horus were worshipped as a trinity or Holy Family. Osiris became god of the dead, Horus his reborn self, and Isis the ideal loving wife and mother.

Robert Graves suggests that the image of the Madonna and Child in Christianity was originally modeled on Isis and Horus as Mother and Son with absent Father. Joseph Campbell likewise speaks of the connection between the statue of the Madonna and Child in the Cathedral of Chartres and the image of Isis and her child. Campbell quotes from the text where the early church fathers make this connection themselves, stating that Christianity superseded the earlier myths.

Obviously the Egyptian myth is a story to explain the rising and falling of the Nile River, which brings a fertile and a dry period to the Egyptian soil. Apart from this seasonal aspect of the myth, it also has deeper psychological implications. Set, ruler of the barren desert (he and Nephthys had no children), driven by the unproductive emotion of jealousy, seeks to thwart the fruitfulness of the land, which represents the loving union of Isis and Osiris. During Isis' search for Osiris, we are told that the land was not fertile. Her devoted love which searched out the wounded part of herself and restored it to a new form of energy in the child Horus is not only an expression of the rebirth of the land. It is also an amazing parallel of the therapeutic process in which one patiently goes through suffering and grieving to find that lost part of oneself in grief or despair. Sometimes it is recovered temporarily, only to be lost or broken again, as Osiris was. Yet loving persistence can create miracles, and the miracle of Isis' love is the regeneration of the lost Osiris into the new-born persona of Horus, who was not only the resurrected Osiris, but a new manifestation later associated with the life-giving Sun. The Son Horus becomes the Sun God, a source of life itself.

The new energy that can arise from the patient loving part of oneself that does not desert us in a time of trouble does indeed seem like a miracle. We have all seen such instances of resurrection in ourselves and others after a difficult time. To have wasted energy blaming Set for his cruelty or Osiris for his foolishness in stepping into a coffin would have accomplished little except to magnify the grief. Similarly, to put ourselves or others down when we are hurting accomplishes little. To let the tears flow, express the sadness, and seek to heal the broken part of ourselves is the feminine principle reasserting balance and ultimately producing the new balanced energy once again. This is fertility in psychological terms. It is the true mating of the masculine and the feminine within.

Perhaps this is why Isis has become the great symbol of the Feminine throughout human history. Hera pales beside her, a pathetic downgraded aspect of the once revered and holy Isis, who expressed love in its deepest and most fruitful way. It is no wonder that Christianity later brought her back in the form of the Virgin Mary, her successor portrayed within the framework of Christian theology. Isis became the symbol of the regenerative feminine principle, expressing deep emotion, using her searching intuition to heal and restore fertility to the masculine principle destroyed by an arid urge for control.

An amalgam of various fertility goddesses of the Near East, achieving the highest form of the goddess in the ancient world, Isis went underground herself, so to speak, during the patriarchal period when gods were elevated to the highest authority and goddesses became their less powerful consorts. Her worship became a secret ritual, known as the Mysteries of Isis, which later permeated Gnosticism and various esoteric groups, including the Rosicrucians of today. Public worship of Isis was banished by the Theodosian Law in 426 C.E. Five years later in 431 C.E. the Council of Ephesus proclaimed the Virgin Mary as Theotokos or God bearer, and in 451 C.E. the Council of Chalcedon proclaimed Mary as a perpetual virgin. The need to honor the feminine principle simply appeared in a new guise, albeit a very chaste one in keeping with the asceticism of early Christianity. Christian architecture made this transference not only in the Cathedral of Chartres mentioned earlier. By 500 C.E. the Temple of Isis at Soissons, France was dedicated to the Virgin Mary. Likewise a shrine in Byzantium dedicated to Isis became the Basilica of Mary at Salonika.

The only account of those ancient Mysteries of Isis is in the work of Lucius Apuleius, *Metamorphoses*, which also contains the story of Psyche and Eros. As an initiate in the second century of the Common Era, Lucius Apuleius could not reveal the Mysteries directly, but his account disguised in this bawdy, satirical tale, popularly known as *The Golden Ass*, is believed to contain a metaphorical description of his own initiation. The hero of the story goes through a series of farcical episodes which parallel the testing and trials of the individual seeking to renounce the lower material life and embrace a higher spiritual awareness symbolized by union with the goddess. To the uninitiated it was simply a comic, picaresque tale not likely to be censured for heresy. To those who understood, it was a metaphor for the process of spiritual enlightenment. Whether she is called Beatrice by Dante, Mary by Christianity or by her many other names, Isis is the Yin of the universe and continues to reassert herself in civilization.

Aphrodite became the love and beauty aspect of Isis in Greek mythology, but lacked her loyalty, which was split off and given to Hera. Able to inspire love primarily on the physical level, Aphrodite lacked the spiritual qualities of Isis. She and her son Eros are both associated with romantic inspiration and the creative principle to a lesser degree. Aphrodite does become the impetus for Psyche's growth in her pursuit of Eros, as we shall see in that story. Hera became the marriage aspect of Isis, honored for her championship of loyalty in partnership, but mated to a controlling, capricious husband who thwarted her ideals and enraged her into jealous vengeance, bringing out the destructive feminine instead of the nurturing one.

Demeter took on the nurturing role and became the fertility goddess in Greece, faithfully searching for her abducted daughter Persephone, but she was subject to Zeus' ruling on Persephone's return from Hades. It is, however, her grieving and withdrawing of fertility from the land that finally brings Zeus to change his mind. In Greece the male principle has the final say. As with Isis, Demeter's followers developed the Eleusinian Mysteries around her story to celebrate the rebirth of the seasons and vegetation. These too were kept secret, known only to the initiates. There seems to be no surviving account of them. All we know from the Homeric Hymn is that the initiate was a person who never again had fear of death. It is as if the ancients knew that the rebirth of the soul is one that must be undertaken individually and quietly. It is not a public act. It is an interior way, the receptive way of the feminine that unites with the outer ego to produce a higher selfhood.

Persephone and Hades: Love in the Underworld

The Greek version of the rebirth of the seasons is the tale of Demeter's daughter Persephone and Hades. Again we have an act of masculine violence precipitating it. This time it is not murder of a brother, but abduction and rape of a niece. It seems that Hades, God of the Underworld and brother of Zeus and Demeter, cast his eye upon the lovely Persephone, daughter of Zeus and Demeter as she came into adolescence and desired her for his wife. Knowing that Demeter, Goddess of the Harvest and adoring mother, would object to her beloved daughter being married to the Underworld, he got Zeus' permission to obtain her in his own way. Already in those days the hierarchy knew how to close ranks and achieve control by deceiving the feminine element.

One day as Persephone in typical adolescent fashion strayed from her mother to follow her own interests, she was drawn to the flaming beauty of a brilliant red flower far afield from mother's watchful eye. Hades had, of course, planted the provocative incentive and was waiting nearby. Excited in her admiration of its fiery beauty, Persephone crouched low to examine the flower. As she did so, the earth opened up and Hades sprang forth with his chariot, scooping up the frightened maiden and carrying her back into the underworld with him. The crack in the earth sealed over, and the only one who witnessed the scene was the sun, Helios.

Back in his own territory, where he was the acknowledged power, Hades felt sure he would have no trouble convincing Persephone and achieving his purpose. Persephone felt otherwise, as the feminine principle often does when peremptorily ordered around by the masculine. Representing the innocent maiden aspect of femininity, Persephone was not ready for this violent encounter with the masculine. Nor was she ready to be rushed into sexual maturity, preferring to choose her own suitor. She withdrew into passive resistance and retreated into herself, refusing to speak.

    This is the other side of the wounded feminine - a paralysis of energy rather than the vengeful fury of Hera. Isis was carried through her grief by a sense of resoluteness fired by her devotion to her mate. Persephone had not had a chance to mature into that kind of love. Rape is insensitive to the internal process of the victim. It forces its own needs upon the other abruptly, concerned only with its own sense of power. On a deeper level, this is the abrupt initiation of the innocent part of ourselves into the adult experience of physical passion which happens to all persons in the process of maturity and forces us to relate to another, whether pleasurably or painfully. With this new awakening came confusion for Persephone and a desire to retreat to the familiar safety of her nurturing mother, Demeter. The awesome responsibility of partnership with the King of the Underworld did not appeal to an unprepared maiden who still needed to form her own identity apart from her overprotective mother. She could not respond to Hades and his offer of queenship in his kingdom, for it was not a free choice growing up from within, but imposed from without.

Many initiations in life are of this sort. We do not seek them; they are thrust upon us before we are ready. The death of a loved one, an unwanted sexual encounter, an unexpected illness or disability can overtake us at any time. And in confusion we sometimes retreat into ourselves. There is a shutting down of energy; joy disappears and despair overcomes. It is an emotional winter, paralleled by the shutting down of growth in the natural world outside. The Greeks said that Demeter caused the shutdown of nature by her grief over losing her child, and thus they explained the barrenness of winter.

According to the myth, Demeter wandered the earth disconsolately in search of Persephone until she met up with Hecate, the wise old goddess often associated with the underworld, representing the intuitive wisdom of age. Hecate suggested she ask Helios the sun, for he sees everything. Helios told Demeter what had happened, but being a good old boy himself, tried to console her with the comment that the King of the Underworld was a good catch for her daughter and was not to be disdained. Obviously he did not comprehend the emotional content of the drama, only the practical analytical side. Going at once to Zeus to demand the return of Persephone and being rebuffed, Demeter began to realize that the male hierarchy was not concerned with the feelings of the ones they had deceived, but were instead congratulating themselves that they were in control. Her response was to withdraw her nurturing and sustenance from the world that depended on her for survival. She retreated to Eleusis to wait out Zeus' change of mind. Possibly this is the first hunger strike in the history of the world, and eventually it produced the desired result. It is not much fun even for the king of the gods, to rule a world that is drying up for lack of nourishment.

In a story modeled upon Isis' search for Osiris, Demeter became nursemaid to the royal child at the Palace of Eleusis and similarly tried to give the child immortality by placing him in the fire. She too is interrupted by the child's mother and reveals herself as the grieving goddess. It is easy to see the influence of the Egyptian myth on the Greek. However, Demeter remained in Eleusis, where a temple was built for her, and it became the center of her worship.

But we are here concerned with Persephone and the depression she experienced by her underground initiation. Psychologically the underworld represents the unconscious part of us and it is always a shock to discover the passions and forces buried there that our innocent self would rather not know. An abrupt encounter with that hidden part of ourselves can be overwhelming when we are not prepared. When we have learned to become familiar with the symbols of the unconscious, making friends with them through our dreams or active imagination, getting in touch with them gradually through therapy or a perceptive friend or partner, we can absorb them into our experience of life without being overwhelmed by them and find a new role for that energy in our lives.

Since Persephone did absorb part of the Underworld by eating some pomegranate seeds there, it was impossible for her to go back to her original innocence with mother. Likewise it was impossible for her to revert to virginity again. Therefore when Zeus finally hearkened to Demeter's anguished demand for the return of her daughter, Persephone was still required to enact her new role as Queen of the Underworld part of the time.

As a nature myth explaining the seasons, the resolution was that she should spend half the year above ground, when Demeter in her joy would bring forth fruit and vegetables on the earth, and half of the year in the Underworld with Hades, when Demeter mourns for her and vegetation ceases to grow. In fact, Persephone is hence forward known as Queen of the Underworld and seems to be there most of the time, figuring in that role in other myths, as we shall see with Psyche.

Thus Persephone, the innocent one rudely initiated into the underworld of the unconscious, matures into the Queen of the Underworld, the feminine partner who welcomes and guides others into the unconscious. When the intuitive process is acknowledged and honored, it can be our greatest guide into the strange world of the unconscious. Hades, the dark passion that rules by physical force, has no subtlety, but when balanced by the intuitive feminine principle of receptivity, can welcome us into the deeper experiences necessary for true maturity. Before her abduction, Persephone was happy and unaware. Hades initiated a new awareness in her, and when Hades and Persephone are in balance, they provide an opportunity for growth during those times of descent into the depths.

People undergoing near-death experiences often report seeing a welcoming white light signaling an entrance to a new plane of existence. Such people are often thrust into near-death by a sudden shocking physical experience such as an accident or heart attack. Hades can still be abrupt, but Persephone's grace lights the way and opens up new levels of experience. Interestingly enough, many of the people feel transformed by their near death encounter and return to ordinary life with a desire to be a guide for others in facing death and in facing life in a new way. Whether it is physical death or death of the ego and awakening to a planetary, unitary consciousness, Hades and Persephone together offer us new depths of awareness.

Another side of this story begs attention. Persephone's close link to her Mother eventually associated her in a three-fold aspect of the feminine known as maiden, mother and crone or as youth, maturity and old age. In this triad Persephone is the maiden, Demeter the mother and Hecate the crone. Hecate was associated with the underworld and the dark side of life. She is usually represented as the older woman who has known both the bright and dark sides of life and represents the wisdom of age. It was she who took Demeter to Helios to discover Persephone's whereabouts. Thus she is the dark wisdom that seeks out reality.

This three-fold concept parallels and predates the patriarchal Trinity of Christianity, with its Father, Son and Holy Spirit. In both cases, three expresses a unity of the divine. Today the Holy Spirit is often being interpreted as the feminine aspect of Christianity, the wisdom of Sophia, bringing a balance to the masculine emphasis. In ancient times, the trinity was associated also with the phases of the moon, in its waxing, full and waning stages. When referring to the lunar cycle, however, the Greeks substituted the moon goddesses Artemis and Selene and retained Hecate in their moon trinity.

These feminine triads represent the Yin polarity, whether it is seen in the lunar stages of the moon, the major chronological stages of life or the vegetation cycle of blossoming spring, the ripe harvest and the barren period of winter. As such, Persephone is also associated with the Eleusinian mysteries developed at Eleusis, the place where Demeter retreated to await the return of Persephone and where a temple was built in honor of her tribulation. We do not know much about the Eleusinian Mysteries, for they were known only to the initiates. We do know that the initiates were said to have transcended all fear of death.

Artemis and Apollo: Sister and Brother

There was one male-female association in Greek mythology that was not romantic in nature, yet also expressed the Yin/Yang polarities. That was the brother and sister combination of Apollo, God of the Sun, and Artemis, Goddess of the Moon. Twin offspring of Zeus and Leto, they had a strong familial bond and complemented one another in their aspects. Artemis represented chastity; she was one of the so-called "virgin goddesses" who was self-sufficient, independent and followed her own course, never paired romantically with anyone. Apollo had love affairs and various children, but never married. Each twin represents a certain independence, yet they also complement each other as two recognized parts of a whole.

Artemis was also goddess of the hunt, and her domain was the wilderness, where she was in charge of wild beasts. Apollo was the god of learning and intellect; his domain was the city and civilization. Artemis ruled the night—the mysterious unknown—the unconscious. Apollo ruled the day, the clear light of rationality, the conscious. In them we have the polarities of light and dark, conscious and unconscious.

Their mother Leto was the daughter of Titans and was one of those unfortunate women on whom Zeus forced his attentions. Hera was particularly vicious towards those lovers of Zeus who conceived children, so Leto not only had to deal with rape by Zeus, but also with a difficult pregnancy decreed by Hera. As soon as she realized Leto was pregnant, Hera sent the serpent python to pursue her from place to place and decreed she must give birth in a place where the sun did not shine. Because everyone feared Hera's jealous wrath, no one would aid the pregnant Leto. She fled to the barren island of Delos finally, where she gave birth first to Artemis and several days later to Apollo. Legend tells us that this once rocky island then flourished with vegetation after the birth of the twins. This metaphor of the island suggests the flowering of life that comes from the act of their birth, i.e. the acknowledgement of both polarities.

In the story of their birth, Artemis preceded Apollo just as unconscious awareness precedes a state of consciousness. She was born at dusk, the time of balance between day and night, when the moon is starting to rise. Apollo was born nine days later after a long and severe labor wreaked upon Leto by the jealous Hera. According to the myth, Artemis in pity on her mother, turned around and assisted her in the long and arduous birth of Apollo. This myth expresses beautifully how the unconscious can aid us, as no one else can, in bringing awareness to light when we are in tune with it and allow it to assist our growth. Consciousness is not a state easily attained. It takes effort and labor to bring awareness into our clear consciousness, particularly if intense emotion (Hera's jealousy) impedes the process of rational thinking.

In actuality both Artemis and Apollo probably came to the Olympian pantheon as Greek representations of far more ancient and archetypal celestial deities from other cultures. Artemis was originally an aspect of the ancient three-fold Triple Goddess representing the three cycles of the moon -

waxing, full and waning. She was sometimes associated with the other moon goddesses, Selene and Hecate in this triple moon aspect. While she eventually came to be the primary moon goddess of the Greeks, Selene remained a minor moon goddess. Hecate, who represented the waning moon or the later stage of life, became known as goddess of the mysterious side of life—the dark underworld aspect. She is also associated with the older woman, crone stage of life in the maiden-mother-crone trinity with Demeter and Persephone. Whereas the original three-fold Triple Goddess had been very powerful in the Near East cultures, this entire moon - life cycle was condensed by the Greeks into one goddess who became a twin to the sun god Apollo.

Apollo was the Greek version of an ancient solar deity who was known by various names in many cultures. The sun was a natural powerful object of worship in primitive times. Apollo is often pictured with his golden chariot making the rounds from east to west as the sun rose and set. To the Greeks, though, he was much more than a solar deity. They associated the light of consciousness with the intellect, the mental faculty, and the civilizing gifts it brought in the way of science and the arts. He had a special friendship with the nine muses, representing the arts, which he brought from their home on Mount Helicon to his shrine at Delphi. He was also especially noted as a musician, particularly for his skill on the lyre, which he had acquired from Hermes, its inventor. He was later the father of Asclepius, God of medicine and healing. Apollo, therefore, represents all the civilizing influences just as Artemis represents the wild, untamed wilderness.

One of Apollo's first deeds was to seek out and punish the python which Hera had sent to hound his mother Leto. The python resided in the Oracle of Mother Earth at Delphi, where she represented the serpentine wisdom. After dispatching the python, Apollo claimed the Delphic Oracle as his own, and ever since he has also been known as the god of prophecy or truth. The priestess of his oracle, known as the Pythoness, reputedly always gave the truth to seekers of answers, even though it might be disguised in a very cryptic answer. This mythological takeover of the revered Delphic Oracle from the primitive Earth Mother is often interpreted as another triumph of the patriarchy in Greece, appropriating the sacred prophetic function for the masculine.

Despite his association with truth and intellect, Apollo had a cruel streak in him, as did Artemis. They had a fierce family loyalty to their mother because of her earlier suffering, and this sometimes produced more passion than wisdom. The indiscrete Niobe made the mistake of boasting that she was superior to Leto because she had produced six beautiful daughters and six handsome sons, while Leto had produced only one of each. Leto asked the twins to avenge her. They did so with fury in a tragic example of overkill. With a torrent of arrows, Apollo slew all six sons and Artemis destroyed all the daughters. Weeping inconsolably, Niobe was turned into a weeping pillar of stone. This vengeful act is memorialized in a famous scene on an ancient Greek terracotta urn.

This inborn family loyalty brought its own kind of grief to them too. Artemis, although dedicated to chastity and forsworn to men, did have a favorite male hunting companion named Orion. A platonic relationship based on love of the hunt characterized their friendship. Nevertheless, Apollo was jealous of Orion, feeling that he himself should be the only male to have a special relationship with the chaste Artemis. Fearing that Artemis might be more influenced by Orion than himself, Apollo arranged for a scorpion to pursue Orion. Unable to kill it with his arrows, Orion dashed into the sea and swam far from land to escape it. Apollo challenged Artemis to see if she could shoot an arrow at that dark speck of his head bobbing in the distance. Always eager to prove her superior skill with bow and arrows, Artemis unknowingly took the bait and sent forth a deadly arrow. It struck Orion's head and killed him instantly.

When Artemis discovered that her own arrow had destroyed her valued companion, she was distraught with grief. She placed Orion among the stars, where he is still pursued in his constellation by the Scorpion and accompanied by his hunting dog, Sirius—the Dog Star.

Artemis too had her streak of cruelty. When the hunter Actaeon accidentally stumbled upon her and her nymphs bathing in the woods, his youthful gawking offended the goddess so much that she turned him into a stag, and his own hunting dogs tore him into pieces. This is more than maidenly modesty. It is an inability to be seen naked, to be viewed as vulnerable by the masculine. In her twinship with Apollo, Artemis rightly emphasized her equal strength and skill, but sometimes lost touch with compassion and an understanding of vulnerability. While Artemis' own sense of completeness did not allow the opening to the masculine energy from without, she would get tied up in her own isolation and competitiveness.

Apollo, in his turn, had no lasting love relation to unite the feminine energy with his mental outlook. He too remained independent, although he had various love affairs and fathered several children. He ruled in his sphere of influence and Artemis ruled in hers without dynamic interplay of the two energies. Each one represented the purity of their individual polarity.

As such, they demonstrate something of Jung's concept of the animus and anima. Although we all have masculine and feminine energy in us, social conditioning often does not allow us to acknowledge the aspects of the opposite gender within us. In Jung's theory the elements characterizing our polar opposite sexual aspects are often the least understood within us. Thus a man's anima is his unacknowledged feminine or Yin aspect, which includes the feeling mode. And a woman's animus is her masculine or Yang side of judgment and discrimination that she may choose to ignore. Whenever we are not in touch with these aspects and they remain blind forces within us, they tend to emerge in inappropriate ways and we are at their mercy. A woman at the mercy of her unacknowledged animus, or the faculty of discrimination, may tend to be dogmatic in her opinions or strident in her demands. Artemis was completely dogmatic in her demand of chastity among her nymphs and treated them cruelly if she discovered them to be otherwise. She also demanded chastity of her devotees as well, leading to difficulties for many other followers.

When a man is obsessed by the anima energy of emotions he is not in touch with he is sometimes moody or sulky and at the mercy of feelings his mind has not integrated. Apollo's jealous treatment of Orion was inappropriate to the situation, but came to the surface when he felt threatened by a rival in influencing his sister. Apollo was also jealous of the satyr Marsyas, whose renowned musical ability brought comparison with Apollo. Challenging Marsyas to a musical contest, Apollo won it and then ignobly and unsportsmanlike flayed the satyr to death.

Artemis sent the dreaded Calydon Boar to ravage the countryside when the king of Calydon forgot to include her in his yearly sacrifices to the twelve gods of Olympus. This seems an over-reaction to an unintended slight. It did lead to one of the most dramatic boar hunts in mythology and also to tragedy for the royal family. But it is another example of overkill. The rage of both Artemis and Apollo at Niobe's children shows something out of control. Neither one has integrated his/her opposite side and so is subject to the unconscious push and pull of those opposite qualities within, leading at times to rash acts and inappropriate deeds.

Apollo's relationship with the Muses and the Pythoness is an interesting one in this regard. In her noted work, *Anima and Animus* Emma Jung, wife of Carl Jung, points out that the Pythoness and the Muses represent anima characteristics, as they mediate between the conscious and the unconscious either through prophecy or inspiration. Perhaps Apollo's close association with them was the Greek way of attempting to deal with the anima energy. Artemis had few relationships to help her to integrate her animus energy, except for Orion, and that was short-lived. In their striking example of the polarities, however, and in their familial bonding, we see clearly that both Apollo and Artemis are a vital part of the universe and of human experience. We can choose to express a single, pure archetype of either one, or to attempt to discover and integrate the presence of the opposite within us also.

Aphrodite and Her Lovers: Love and War and Others

No discussion of love would be complete without Aphrodite herself, Goddess of Love and Beauty. As mentioned before, she does not really encompass the totality of love, but rather the aspect of sexual attraction. This is natural in that she is a later, more civilized version of the Earth Mother whose primary urge is procreation and assuring the continuity of life. Aphrodite was the Greek refinement of that ancient belief that required the great goddess to mate with a male consort annually to ensure the fertility of the land. Centuries earlier, in countries to the east of Greece, she was called Inanna in Sumeria, Ishtar in Babylonia and Astarte in Phoenicia. They each had an annual consort who died after the spring mating to ensure new virility for the following year.

That actual sacrifice of the male consort was practiced originally in early cultures seems to be an accepted fact now. Later the sacrifice became more symbolic, with an animal and still later ceremonial ritual replacing the sacrifice itself. Patriarchal society may well have arisen partly as a natural revolt against this practice. Or in psychological terms, the ego came to assert its freedom from the demand of the primitive fertility that sacrificed independent will for the collective continuation.

Hence to the later patriarchal Greeks, for whom the development of the individual mind and intellect was so important, Aphrodite was the civilized representation of that ancient fertility goddess. The emphasis, however, was on the physical love and attractiveness that appealed to the Greeks' aesthetic sense without threatening their intellectual development. The nurturing characteristic was given to Demeter, where emphasis was on the maternal. Dividing the original goddess in this way removed the threat to the patriarchal development of the ego and yet also assured a place for the vital principle of attraction so necessary for continuation of the species.

So Aphrodite represents the physical love and beauty that undergirds the attraction of the sexes. As such, she cannot be limited to one consort, but must spread her favors over an assortment, including both gods and mortals. Aphrodite is a delightful goddess whom we all enjoy experiencing. She is that rush of joy that comes with initial attraction and adds so immeasurably to our lives. She can also bring pain when the attraction ebbs or turns sour in imbalance. The stories about her portray both joy and pain.

Although later versions attribute her fatherhood to Zeus, the earlier version is that she arose naked from the foam of the sea, riding on a scallop shell and landed on the island of Cyprus. This is the familiar image portrayed by Botticelli in his famous painting, The Birth of Venus expressing Aphrodite's exquisite grace and beauty. She would, of course, have come from the earlier civilizations to the east, but the watery element of the sea also appropriately implies the emotional nature of her essence.

Hesiod's version is that her birth was generated by a mixture of sea and sperm from the genitals of Uranus when

Cronos castrated his father and threw his phallus into the sea. From the foam that arose, Aphrodite emerged full grown. Some say that her son Eros accompanied her at her beginning; others claim his father to be Ares, Hermes or even Zeus. As the male form of the primordial sexual force, Eros is always associated with Aphrodite. Since the Yin energy is that of bringing together, while the Yang is that of individuation, the feminine representation is the primordial one, with the male aspect acknowledged as her son. That is why the original Great Goddess in earlier cultures often had a son/lover as her annual sacrificial consort. The son of the ritual mating became the new consort after the sacrifice of the old to ensure perpetual virility. By the time of the Greeks, the son had become the perpetual, somewhat effeminate youth Eros, whose immature behavior and irresponsible passion often had disturbing and chaotic results. Thus the Greeks express their philosophy of the need for reasoned balance in all things. Today Eros is our sentimental Cupid. In one story, however, he did mature, as we shall see in the later story of Psyche and Eros, where he was able to become a more stable partner.

Aphrodite herself was never a stable partner, although married to the lame Hephaestus, God of Fire and the Forge. The implications of this union are that physical love does indeed contain sparks of fire. Also the quickening inspiration of Aphrodite can inspire the craftsmanship of Hephaestus at the forge. On a more subtle level, I suspect that promiscuity prefers a mate unable to keep up with her many quick and lively assignations that are essential to her essence. The intense incendiary nature of her attraction can burn itself out quickly if not sustained by other qualities. Hence she and Hephaestus had no children, no extension of their connection into another generation.

She had a much more passionate relationship with Ares, God of War and brother of her husband Hephaestus. A strange combination this may seem, of Love and War; yet the Greeks were inevitably perceptive. Both are intense passions. Love can turn violent, as the battered woman syndrome attests, and violence can sometimes be tamed by love. They had three children who illustrate both possibilities. Their two sons, Deimos (Terror) and Phobos (Fear), were natural results of the former. Their mother more or less withdrew and left them to their father, who took them into battle with him. After all, fear and terror can only thrive in the absence of love. Ares and Aphrodite did also produce a daughter Harmonia, which may seem a bit odd. Yet harmony can result when the two passions of love and war are in proper balance.

This mating with violence, however passionate it was, came to a disastrous end when Hephaestus finally realized over the years that something was going on. He fashioned a fine golden net and secretly attached it to Aphrodite's bed. Saying he would be away at his forge for awhile, he hid and waited until he caught Aphrodite and Ares together in bed. Entangled in the golden net, they could not escape and were held up to ridicule by Hephaestus, who summoned the other gods to view their embarrassment and his outrage.

Although that may have ended the affair with Ares, Aphrodite's promiscuity was not curtailed by this rude public disclosure, and she continued to express her nature freely.

From her union with Poseidon, god of the sea, came Rhodos after whom the island of Rhodes is named. From her union with Hermes, the messenger god came the bisexual Hermaphrodite, a combination of both their sexes and a fitting son of the god who could communicate well with all and change a story to suit the hearer.

One of her most famous children was Aeneas, whom she bore to the mortal Anchises, shepherd king of the Dardanians, allies of Troy. Taken with an instant fancy to the handsome shepherd, she seduced him on a hillside and bore from that union their son Aeneas of whom she was very proud. When Aeneas aided the Trojans in their war with the Greeks, he was the only Trojan champion to escape unscathed from Troy. Aphrodite protected him in battle and led him, with his crippled father, safely from the burning Troy, guiding him to Italy, where he became the legendary founder of Rome. The goddess lost interest in Anchises after he boasted of having enjoyed her and was crippled by a thunderbolt from Zeus. It was the son and his new energy that interested her, not the aging and crippled father. Impulsive, momentary passion seldom survives the ravages of time and infirmity.

The Trojan War is an instance illuminating her irresponsibility for events she set in action. Finding herself at odds with Hera in the Trojan War, Aphrodite had little effect on the Trojan War once she set it in action by giving Helen of Sparta to Paris of Troy as a bribe in the beauty contest, thus breaking the marriage bond between Helen and her husband Menelaus. She was no help to Paris afterward or to the other Trojans except for her own son Aeneas. Sexual attraction without commitment takes no responsibility for the consequences of its actions.

One of the goddess' most interesting and complex relationships was with Adonis, an exceedingly handsome mortal. His very birth was orchestrated by Aphrodite when a mortal woman boasted that her daughter was more beautiful than Aphrodite. The goddess' revenge was to make the daughter fall in love with her own father, King of Cyrmias and consummate it one night when he was drunk. Afterward, when he realized that he was both father and grandfather of his daughter's unborn child; he chased her from the palace, intent on killing her. Aphrodite changed her into a myrrh tree, which her father's sword split in two, and out tumbled the beautiful infant Adonis. Repenting her impulsive mischief, Aphrodite placed Adonis in a chest and gave it to Persephone for safe keeping in the underworld. Out of curiosity Persephone opened the chest and was so intrigued by the golden haired child that she lifted him out and raised him in her own palace.

When he matured, he became her lover. Upon hearing of this, Aphrodite realized she had missed a good thing and immediately went to Zeus to demand equal time with Adonis. In another instance of cowardice in the face of feminine competition, Zeus transferred the matter to the Muses, who decided Adonis should spend a third of the year with each of the goddesses and a third by himself. Not satisfied with only a third of the year, Aphrodite pursued him also during his own third of the year as well. This third he liked to spend going hunting and Aphrodite would warn him often to avoid ferocious beasts for fear of an accident.

One day while hunting he wounded a wild boar (which some say was the jealous Ares in disguise). Turning on him, the boar gored him to death and savagely tore his handsome body to pieces. Now it seemed he would be in the underworld all of the time. Aphrodite pleaded with Zeus to allow him to return to her just for the summer months, and this time Zeus acquiesced.

Here we have the Greek version of the seasonally dying lover tradition from the ancient Near East. In fact the name of the annual lover of the earlier Phoenician goddess Astarte was Adonis. There are also similarities to the Osiris story here. It is interesting that the Greeks made this story into a triangle involving Persephone, who is herself part of a seasonal cycle myth. In this sophisticated version, it is the misdirected power of love (incest caused by a revengeful Aphrodite) that brings the youth to birth, the compassionate intuition of Persephone who sees his potential and brings him to maturity, the erotic greed of Aphrodite and the backlash of a former jealous lover of hers that lead to his death, and the renewing power of sexual love that brings about his annual resurrection. There was in fact a whole cult built around Adonis' story of death and return. Today we know his name mainly as an adjective for a sexually attractive, exceptionally good-looking young man.

While Aphrodite is indeed the energizing and renewing aspect of love and much to be desired, she is often at the mercy of raw emotion as well. Her emotional response to any threatened rival in beauty reveals itself in her revenge on the hapless mother of Adonis and again in the story of Psyche. She can bring pain to relationship as well as bliss, particularly when jealousy enters in. Angered at the refusal of the handsome Hippolytus, son of Theseus, to honor her because he was sworn to chastity in honor of Artemis, she brought about his downfall by causing his stepmother Phaedra to fall in love with him. Phaedra too was destroyed by her unrequited love, and Theseus plunged into despair over the both of them. Aphrodite provided the impetus for Medea to fall in love with Jason in his quest of the Golden F1eece, but the very intensity and possessiveness of that love also helped to destroy the relationship, for it lacked a stabilizing element.

It is as an initiator of new energy that Aphrodite functions best. As such we all welcome her influence, but we must ground that energy in appropriate ways for lasting satisfaction. Those in her thrall will be at the mercy of her short-lived intensity. They may find themselves constantly craving new adventures in love or the continuous high of drug-induced intoxication.

Aphrodite can bring renewal to us, but we must go deeper than her initial impulse. Hers is a love based on sexual attraction. Passionate and intense, it is usually temporary. Even her beloved Adonis is only temporary in its seasonal arrangement. Then she is on to another conquest. It was up to her daughter-in- law Psyche to raise love to a new level of commitment by growing through a series of trials into a deeper, more complete expression of love with Eros.

Interestingly, it was Aphrodite who set in motion these trials for Psyche, which we will explore in a later chapter.

Jason and Medea: Quest of the Golden Fleece

Some of the mortals in Greek mythology had relationships also worth viewing from the perspective of polarities. These stories bring us into the realm of the hero rather than the gods. With the hero, we are dealing not with a powerful archetypal force, but rather the untried or unawakened soul coming into its own. In each of the following stories this maturing requires a uniting of masculine and feminine energy to accomplish the initiatory task. We will be looking in these stories at the way in which the emerging hero, which can be interpreted as the emerging ego of any of us, deals with the feminine energy it encounters in this process. One of the most dramatic of these stories is that of Jason and Medea.

We are all familiar with the classic heroic journey or quest where the young hero needs to prove himself worthy to be an adult or worthy to rule a kingdom. To keep this from a gender-based approach, let us interpret the kingdom as being our own lives, and the fitness to rule as the maturity to take charge of our own lives. Each one of us is the hero/heroine on our own, personal journey to maturity. Heroes must always go through certain rites of passage or testing, like the knights of King Arthur, in order to show their courage, strength, and wisdom. Thus the story of Jason and Medea is also the story of the Quest for the Golden Fleece.

Beginnings are important in mythology, so let us digress to the origin of the Golden Fleece to fully understand this particular quest. There once was a king in Thessaly named Athamas, who grew tired of his first wife by whom he had two children named Phrixus and Helle, so he cast her aside and married another. When the new wife produced her own heir to the throne, she plotted to get Phrixus and Helle out of the way in order that her son would have no rivals. Deciding that their sacrifice could be demanded by a draught in the land, she secretly parched all the corn, before it was sown one year, and the expected draught occurred from lack of harvest. She then saw to it that the oracles demanded the sacrifice of Phrixus and Helle, and the king sadly agreed. An oracle could not be disobeyed.

On the day of the sacrifice, the children's real mother prayed to the gods to save them. Just as the axe was about to strike, Hermes as messenger of the gods appeared with a ram of golden fleece which sprang into the air with the two children on its back. This story may have its precedent in the Hebrew tale of Abraham and Isaac, where a ram is sent by God to spare the sacrifice of Isaac. The golden ram of Hermes flew east over the Black Sea. Unfortunately there Helle fell off and gave her name to the Hellespont, her only claim to immortality. Phrixus hung on until the ram landed in Colchis at the far end of the Black Sea. To the patriarchal Greeks the loss of the female child would be less significant than loss of the male. This loss of the feminine energy, however, sets a tone for the entire adventure. It is lack of a balanced feminine energy that characterizes the quest and determines its tragic ending.

In Colchis Phrixus sacrificed the ram to Zeus and hung the golden fleece in a sacred grove, guarded by an unsleeping dragon. Hence it becomes a valuable treasure, difficult to steal. Since the ram represents a divine power capable of saving the children from a life-threatening situation, the fleece, a symbol of that power, now represents a hidden treasure or hidden power. The golden color suggests a connection with solar power or mind, implying a fully awakened consciousness, not something easily attained. Having thus discharged his duty to the gods, Phrixus settled down in Colchis and later married a daughter of the king.

Meanwhile, back in Thessaly his kinsmen Pelias and Aeson were contesting for a neighboring kingdom. The wily Pelias out maneuvered Aeson, who gave up the throne on the condition that his son Jason should have it when he came of age. To protect Jason from his crafty uncle, the child was sent by Aeson to the mountains to be reared by Chiron, the famous Centaur who fostered various other heroes such as Hercules and Achilles.

At the age of twenty, Jason was told by an oracle to go back and reclaim the throne from his uncle. On the way back to the city, he had various adventures to test his strength and nobility. Just before entering the city he had to cross a swift-flowing river. An old woman who was Hera in disguise tested him by begging his help in crossing the river. He nobly carried her across, passing her test, and thereafter had her help in his exploits. By responding in a compassionate way, he opened himself to the feminine energy and enabled it to aid him.

During the river crossing he lost a sandal in the rushing water. That was how Pelias knew him, for there was a prophecy that a man with one sandal would threaten his kingdom. Being a wily strategist who would do well today in international politics, Pelias did not just kill his rival, but chose a much more subtle way to be rid of him. He told Jason he must first prove himself worthy of kingship through a heroic quest and suggested he find and return the golden fleece of their kinsman Phrixus, saying it rightly belonged in Thessaly. In Pelias' mind this was tantamount to murder, since it was considered an impossible quest.

Jason, however, in his youthful enthusiasm took it on joyfully and made a great expedition out of it. While the ship to be known as the Argo was being built, Jason sent out a call for heroes to join him and ended up with a distinguished crew of Argonauts, including the likes of Hercules, Theseus, Orpheus, Achilles' father and others. On the way they had numerous adventures and weathered them all, sometimes with the aid of Hera. They even managed to escape between the Symplegades, two clashing rocks in the Black Sea that destroyed many boats. Following the advice of an old man, they sent a dove ahead and sped through while the rocks were separating after clashing in on her.

Mircea Eliade has an interesting discussion of the initiatory symbolism of the Symplegades as an image of the difficulties involved in achieving a higher consciousness in his book *Rites and Symbols of Initiation*. He sees them as guardians of a treasure, which can only be achieved if the hero can successfully negotiate opposing forces. Joseph Campbell further interprets the clashing rocks as the major polarities in life, such as good and evil, hope and fear, life and death that must be successfully dealt with by the hero. Since Jason barely squeaked through the Symplegades, with the rocks denting the back part of' his boat, perhaps it is not an unfair assumption that he had not fully mastered the polarities within himself sufficiently to deal with the power he was set on achieving.

Arriving in Colchis, Jason announced himself and made known his request to the king of Colchis, who was not pleased to hear it. Colchis had achieved great fame because of the fleece; doubtless it was a tourist attraction and economic asset. After all, would Paris give up the Eiffel Tower? Being another seasoned statesman, the king agreed to give it up only if Jason performed two impossible tasks. First, he must yoke two fire-breathing bulls and then he must plough the field of Ares with dragon's teeth from which armed soldiers would spring. If he survived the fiery breath of the bulls, he must then defend himself against the rows of soldiers. Recognizing the futility of accomplishing these tasks, Jason knew he needed help and cast his eye on the king's daughter Medea, famed for her sorcery and magical powers. Having experienced success in the seduction of the maidens enroute to Colchis, Jason saw a possible way out of his dilemma. To ensure success for her hero, Hera cajoled Aphrodite into enflaming Medea's heart with love for Jason and a desire to save his life. Jason and Medea met by stealth later that evening, after the banquet for the Argonauts. Seduction worked its will, and Medea provided him with a potion to make him fire-proof against the bulls. She then advised him to throw a stone among the soldiers as they sprang up, and he would be saved.

To the outraged amazement of the king the next day, Jason calmly and safely yoked the ferocious bulls together and began to plough the field. As rows of armed soldiers sprang up from the dragons' teeth, Jason merely tossed a rock among them, and they fell to killing themselves instead of Jason. Shrewd politicians still use this tactic of diversion today. Knowing that Medea's sorcery must have been behind this, the king rushed back to the palace to confront her. She, however, was so enamored of Jason by now that she quickly guided him to the grove where the golden fleece was guarded by the never-sleeping dragon. Crooning a magic lullaby and sprinkling a magic charm on the dragon, Medea eased it to sleep as Jason grabbed the fleece. Together they fled to the Argo, with Medea's little brother in tow.

The dragon is a symbol for the ancient feminine wisdom in many cultures. In this instance, we have the older, deep wisdom of restraint literally being lulled to sleep by glamorous illusions and allowing the higher consciousness of the fleece into hands not ready to receive it and to deal with its power.

Quickly the Argonauts set sail, with the king's fleet in hot pursuit. As the king began to overtake them, Medea's burning desire to be with Jason reached a peak of cold-blooded calculation. Sacrificing her brother for her lover, she hacked her brother's body to pieces and threw them in the sea, knowing full well that her father, out of grief and paternal obligation, would cease the chase to collect his son's body for a proper burial. Thus the Argonauts escaped with the Golden Fleece, gained through sorcery and murder.

After many adventures on the way back, they returned to Thessaly, where Jason was eager to show off his new bride, famed for her sorcery. Seeing his father old and ill, he asked Medea to restore Aeson to youth. This she accomplished by brewing a huge cauldron of herbs and potions, putting Aeson in the cauldron, cutting his throat for the blood to run out and be replaced with the magic potion. When the daughters of Pelias saw the miraculous change in their uncle, they begged Medea to do the same for their father.

Again she brewed a huge caldron, but left out the magic potion. Placing Pelias in it, she told the daughters to cut his throat. To their horror, he collapsed and died in the cauldron. This act, calculated to put Jason on the throne backfired as Jason and Medea were forced to flee from the outrage of the citizens at such a dastardly act. The cauldron of renewal is another ancient symbol, particularly in Celtic mythology, where it represents both the fertile womb and creativity or inspiration. With the contrived death of Pelias, Medea has again misused the feminine energy, making the cauldron a source of destruction rather than renewal, in the name of revenge. Obviously Jason has joined in marriage with an unbalanced feminine energy. Intending to manipulate Medea for his own purposes, she is now manipulating him. And the combination does not bode well for either one. Unbalanced energy breeds more of the same.

Jason and Medea fled to Corinth, where Medea's father had once reigned. There they settled down and had two sons. As time went on, Jason became disenchanted with Medea and her exotic temperament. Viewed with suspicion as a foreigner and a sorceress and with few friends, she clung to him possessively. Finally, given the opportunity to marry the daughter of the king of Corinth, thereby eventually having a kingdom to rule, he turned his back on Medea and married Princess Glauce.

But one does not cast off with impunity a woman as powerful and as possessive in love as Medea. Pretending to accept the situation, she sent a gift of a beautiful robe to the new bride. Into it she had woven a dreadful poison. No sooner had Jason's bride put it on than she began to burn from the poison. As her anguished father tried to pull it off her, he too was burned and both died in horrendous agony. Knowing only too well who was behind this, Jason rushed home to confront Medea. Her mind distorted by jealousy and revenge, she appeared on the roof of their burning home with a knife and their two sons in her arms. Jason pleaded with her to leave him his two sons. She only laughed as she slew them both. Then summoning a magical winged chariot, she rose above the flames of destruction she had wrought and swept off to Athens where she obtained sanctuary by promising to restore youth to King Aegeus, the father of Theseus.

Jason, who had now lost his kingdom and all he loved because of Medea, wandered disconsolately. Finally he went to sit by the Argo in the harbor, vainly trying to recall his days of glory. Ruminating thus, he was killed when the rotting hull of the ship crashed down on him.

From such a promising start in life, what happened to lead to such tragedy? The Golden Fleece is a worthy pursuit, but it is a dangerous one. The goal of inner power or heightened awareness is eagerly sought today too. But when the prize becomes a source of power over others procured by artificial means instead of patiently developing balanced power in harmony with others, through disciplined inner work, it can backfire. When Jason acquired the Fleece, his power of self-realization came by a manipulation of the feminine energy. He relied on Medea's charms and drugs to accomplish his goal without really understanding feminine power. He manipulated Medea through seduction (the power of Aphrodite) to achieve his own goal, not through any inherent love of her. He further accepted her manipulations, including the betrayal of her brother, her father, and Pelias. Once into the spirit of deception, he found it hard to break out until it led to his own deception.

When Jason tired of Medea and tried to cast her aside, her jealous, angry and devouring aspect came out. Alienated and separated from the masculine polarity, distorted feminine energy can become vindictive. Jason made the classic mistake of never taking his feminine side seriously, only using Medea when he needed her. She was an exotic foreigner that he showed off when it suited him and thrust away when she embarrassed him. Theirs was not a true marriage of respect and love; it was a marriage of convenience and manipulation.

In turning to Medea for help, Jason was choosing to engage with a sorceress, a dangerous form of feminine energy, which eventually turned on him and became the source of his own destruction. There are those who feel that Medea has been cast as the perennial witch and her power decried as sorcery in this patriarchal story to excuse Jason from responsibility. The Woman's Encyclopedia of Myths and Secrets describes her simply as the "Wise One" and as a healer.

In her novel, *The Dawn Palace*, H. M. Hoover goes back to sources prior to Euripides' play "Medea" to support her view of Medea as a wise foreigner misunderstood and feared by the Greeks for her power and her challenge to the subservient role of women. Jason is portrayed as an opportunistic villain who slays Pelias and Medea's brother, as well as his own sons, and is thoroughly deserving of his wretched end. This attempt to redress a patriarchal condemnation of Medea creates sympathy for Medea and provides an alternative perspective on the relationship. Hoover even claims that Euripides was paid by the Corinthians to write a play absolving them of responsibility for child murder.

These revisionist interpretations may well be more accurate descriptions of the character of Medea in pre-Greek times. While there may have been a deliberate attempt by the Greek storytellers to exalt their hero Jason at Medea's expense, I see no value in failing to acknowledge that her feminine energy is unbalanced in the Greek story. It is a drama of high potential gone astray in both Jason and Medea precisely because there is no balancing of their energies. Medea had great inner powers of magic and healing that could have enriched their partnership. When rejected by a self-centered partner, she employed that power in destructive ways to revenge her pain. Medea is neither villain nor victim. She is that unbalanced element in ourselves that is hurt if rejected and can push us to irrational behavior. In a man, this could be his anima energy; in a woman it is her Hera side. We have a clue to this in the very beginning when it is Hera whom Jason first encounters as the feminine.

We all have an unbalanced element within us; whether it is fear, jealousy, will to power, anger, or a multitude of other distortions. The more we unconsciously identify with that element in ourselves, the more destructive it becomes in our lives. This is the part of us that Jung termed the shadow. Instead of casting it aside, we need to acknowledge and understand that part of ourselves. Identifying with its distortion or repressing it will not help. We need to understand and respect its misused power in our lives, for it is a potential source of energy. Medea's original potential was that of healing. Transforming and synthesizing that energy in constructive ways can enrich our lives. This is a quest in which we are all engaged. It requires a willingness to tune into the Yin polarity through deep inner work and takes time. Only then can the Golden Fleece rightfully become ours.

Theseus and Ariadne: Love and Abandonment

Another intriguing pair of mortals was Theseus and Ariadne. Theseus was the son of King Aegeus of Athens, the same king who took in Medea hoping she would restore his virility. Theseus also claimed paternity by Poseidon, God of the Sea, which puts him in that class of heroes known as demigods, those having both human and divine parentage. Here is how it happened.

King Aegeus of Athens, sad at being childless, went to visit a neighboring king in Troezen, who had a beautiful daughter named Aethra. While there he was hospitably invited to share Aethra's bed. That same night that she was with Aegeus, however, Aethra is said to have been led in a dream to the temple of Poseidon and to have lain also with the god, by whom she conceived Theseus. Thus does a culture bestow semi-divinity on a popular hero. Athens, being a sea power, would naturally have wanted a personal connection with the god of the sea.

When Aegeus left Troezen, hoping to have fathered a child, he left his sword and sandals under a huge rock with instructions to Aethra that Theseus should be sent to Athens when he was old enough to remove the rock. This test is echoed in Celtic folklore when King Arthur proves he is the Son of Uther Pendragon and hence heir to the throne of Britain by pulling a sword from a stone. Likewise Sir Galahad proves his fitness for the quest of the Holy Grail when he does a similar feat. At age sixteen Theseus was strong enough to move the rock, so his mother sent him to Aegeus in Athens.

Theseus deliberately chose the longest and most difficult route, overthrowing beasts and tyrants along the way, so that his fame preceded him to Athens. Here we have the adolescent hero challenging himself with feats of strength to prove his manhood. Young people often seek out challenges to prove themselves. Society can do them a great service by emphasizing constructive challenges rather than glorifying destructive ones, as the media is sometimes wont to do.

When he arrived in Athens, he was met by Medea who had divined who he was and saw him as a threat to her own influence over the king. She persuaded the king that he was dangerous and offered a cup of poison to Theseus. Just as he was about to drink it, the king recognized his sword and sandals and dashed the cup to the ground, embracing his unknown son. Medea, exposed once again in her jealous, dangerous aspect, called her winged chariot and returned this time to Colchis, where no more is heard of her. Theseus was welcomed royally and proclaimed heir to the throne of Athens.

Shortly thereafter Theseus found an exploit to fully challenge his worthiness to be king, Some years earlier, after losing a sea battle to Crete, the Athenians were forced to pay a tribute to Crete every ninth year in the form of seven youths and seven maidens who were sent to be devoured by the Minotaur. Soon after Theseus' arrival came the time to send the tribute and lots were drawn to determine the youths.

Theseus, full of self confidence, volunteered to go and deliver Athenian youth from their doom. He would slay the Minotaur and end the tribute forever. Here was a worthy challenge! His father tried to dissuade him from going, but when Theseus insisted, he bade him farewell in sorrow and instructed him to change the black sails of the sacrificial ship to white ones if he succeeded.

So Theseus' challenge now was to face the Minotaur, a monster with a man's body and a bull's head who was imprisoned in a labyrinth of many mazes constructed by the famous architect Daedalus. The Minotaur was a great embarrassment to King Minos of Crete, for it was a reminder of his lack of character. While contesting with his brothers for the throne of Crete, Minos had been provided by Poseidon with a magnificent white bull from the sea to acknowledge his kingship. Once proclaimed king, he was to sacrifice the bull to Poseidon. It was such a magnificent animal and would be such an asset in breeding his own stock of bulls that Minos decided to keep it for himself and not honor his commitment to Poseidon. As punishment for this greed and failure to honor a higher power, Poseidon asked Aphrodite to visit Queen Pasiphae with a monstrous passion for the bull, a great embarrassment to Minos. The consummation of that passion produced the Minotaur, who fed on human flesh. Minos had the Labyrinth constructed to conceal this shameful progeny. Each year he fed it the youths of Athens to keep it satisfied, lest it destroy Crete in its rage.

This is most likely a myth to explain a number of historical events. Probably leaders of several cults were contesting for the kingship of Crete, which had formerly been matrilinear. This was a time of transition to patriarchy, and the leader of the bull cult won out by claiming divine acknowledgement and marrying the queen. Excavations in Crete have revealed a hall with a labyrinthan or spiral-like pattern on the floor, probably for a ceremonial dance, which may have given rise to the story of the famous Labyrinth.

When the Athenians arrived at Crete, they were royally entertained at the king's palace before their sacrifice. Theseus told of his adventures and exploits, boasting that he was the son of Poseidon. This was unsettling to Minos, for although head of an island sea power, he had lost favor with Poseidon. To humiliate Theseus he challenged him to retrieve a ring thrown into the sea. Theseus retrieved not only the ring, but also the crown of the sea nymphs, symbolizing his true connection to Poseidon and greater ability to rule.

It happened that Ariadne was at the dinner that night. She was the daughter of Pasiphae and Minos, true heir to the throne of Crete according to matrilinear rule and priestess of the goddess tradition which was vying with the patriarchal cults. Hearing of Theseus' exploits, watching him conduct himself with dignity and nobility, courageously retrieving the ring and crown, she fell in love with him and determined to save him. She went to Daedelus for instructions about the Labyrinth and got from him a ball of twine. Early the next morning she gave the twine to Theseus. He unrolled it in the maze and found his way back to her. She begged him to marry her and take her back to Greece, for her place in Crete had been usurped by Minos.

While the Athenian youths anxiously entered the labyrinth, their hopes pinned on Theseus, Ariadne waited patiently at the entrance, holding the string that would enable them to return. Hearing a noise, Theseus left his companions and went on alone. It was very dark in the maze, and he had to use his sense of hearing and touch to determine where the monster was. Finally he heard a great roar and sensed the presence of the beast directly before him. Taking the bull's head by the horns, he encountered it, succeeded in killing it, and retraced his route with the thread. Ariadne hid them all until dark, when they crept onto the ship in the harbor and set sail for Athens. In their great excitement to get away, they neglected to change the sails to white ones.

Enroute to Athens they stopped for the night on the island of Naxos, where Theseus made love to Ariadne, then left her sleeping and pregnant and sailed away. She awoke, saw the ship on the horizon and knew she was deserted by the one she had loved. All alone, she wept and grieved at this betrayal of trust. When the ship returned to Athens, Aegeus spotted the black sails from a distance. Believing his son dead, Aegeus killed himself in grief by leaping into the Aegean Sea, which now bears his name. Theseus' triumphant arrival was shattered by the news of his father's death. He ascended to the throne with sadness, but ruled Athens with distinction.

This is a myth rich in symbolism. While on the surface, it may have arisen from various historical events and treaties between Greece and Crete, and subsequently a shift in Crete to a patriarchal culture, its deeper significance lies on the psychological level as an initiation story. In contrast to the abrupt initiation of Persephone, this one is consciously chosen and undertaken by the hero as a means of self development. Although the emphasis is on his physical feat, all the elements in the story express deeper truths that resonate in human experience. Mircea Eliade, who has made a thorough exploration of mythic initiations, describes his own life as "ordeal by labyrinth" in his conversations with Claude-Henri Rocquet.

The Minotaur concept may well have originated as a result of Theseus' wrestling match or battle with the bull cult commander and was later magnified into a beast half human and half animal. Whatever its origin, it provides a great challenge for Theseus and makes a dramatic story. On a deeper level, the Minotaur is a reminder of the greed of Minos, the flaw or human weakness that becomes magnified when it is hidden and not acknowledged.

Mythically it represents the failure of Minos to honor the religious element he had called upon for help. The Minotaur, with its animal aspect, is distorted energy that turns destructive.

Labyrinth is the term we sometimes give to the inner ear, with its twists and turns creating the conditions necessary for hearing. Symbolically the labyrinth represents our inner life. Eliade likens the center of the labyrinth to the center of one's being, the zone of the sacred. Finding our center amid the distractions of the twists and turns of life is not easy. But it is in that center that we face our fears and know who we are.

The challenge of the Minotaur, then, is to enter the complex inner labyrinth, overcome the beast or human distortion at the heart of it, and return to outer life in command of ourselves. The Minotaur can live only as long as it is fed by fresh energy, supplied in the myth by Athenian youths. When we cease to feed into these distortions, as Theseus symbolically demonstrated, they lose their hold over us. To overcome that which we most fear to face in ourselves, we must confront it and acknowledge it so that it no longer controls us. This is the challenge awaiting all of us. It is the perilous, yet necessary journey to true self discovery. To submit to the fear of facing our own distorted illusions, recognize them for what they are so that they no longer control us is truly the courageous act that enables us to live consciously and responsibly in the world.

To function within the labyrinth it is necessary to turn to our feminine side of intuition and sensing. In the darkness of the maze, Theseus had to tune into his sense of hearing and touch, relying on his intuition. Ariadne, the feminine guide, joins with Theseus in providing the clue to negotiating the twists and turns with a ball of twine, that steady purpose linking him back to the outer world, so that he is not lost within the inner world. Ariadne is the feminine energy and wisdom that allows access to the inner self, which guides to completion of the task. Motivated by love for the youthful hero (the becoming self), she is the wisdom that allows us to confront the beast of our distorted energy and not be victimized by it. She brings inspiration, encouragement and insight to Theseus' readiness to explore the labyrinth, which is to explore our own soul. Yet she is rejected by Theseus after helping him.

Why did Theseus leave her behind on the island? One version of the myth says that he simply forgot which is rather hard to believe. A more euphemistic version says that the "gods" made him forget. That pathetic excuse assumes tremendous naiveté on the part of Theseus and listener alike, an injustice to both. While it is true that in crises we often make promises to be noble and conveniently "forget" them afterward, this act seems more deliberate.

Theseus chooses to leave his feminine energy behind after it has served its purpose. Ariadne activated the evolvement within him; he is not yet ready to appreciate her and fully acknowledge his feminine side. Basically still a youth, he is not yet ready to commit to his higher self. He wanted freedom to explore, and explore he did. Theseus had many adventures with women and ultimately several wives, including an Amazon who gave him a son Hippolyte. His last wife was Phaedra, sister of Ariadne. As mentioned earlier, Aphrodite caused Phaedra to fall in love with her stepson, Hippolyte, and this led to tragedy for all.

Theseus has come down in legend as an outstanding ruler of Athens, but he eventually lost favor with the people by his treatment of Hippolyte. He left Athens meeting his death at the hands of a jealous king, who pushed him into the sea. In the end the son of Poseidon returned to Poseidon. In his youth, as the slayer of the Minotaur, Theseus is the new energy that confronts a challenge and overcomes the distorted energy of the Minotaur created by the corrupt attitude of King Minos. He is the fresh promise, the true son of Poseidon, that divine element Minos failed to honor. With the aid of Ariadne, he overcomes the monster of corruption and proves himself a fitting energy to rule his kingdom.

He is a more evolved hero than Jason and represents a consciousness more in touch with the feminine. But he was not yet ready for the complete marriage of the masculine and feminine polarities, so he could not permanently honor the feminine even though he opened himself up to it briefly. All his life he was obsessed with adventure, stirring up action wherever he could, and exemplifying the male polarity. There are numerous tales of his later exploits, not all worthy ones by any means. It was while Theseus was away on long exploits, neglecting his wife, Phaedra that she fell in love with her stepson.

Historically Theseus represents the patriarchal approach dominant in Greece and coming to the fore in Crete. Such a hero would have to emphasize the Yang quality of action, as Theseus did all through his life. In the one episode where he encountered the representative of the goddess in Ariadne, we are given a glimpse of the potential when he is in touch with her. That he later abandons her is a statement about that stage of civilization as well as a comment about the desire of the ego to flex its power on its own.

In Theseus' desertion of Ariadne we see civilization leaving behind the old goddess concept and matrilinear rule. The feminine order is no longer valued as a lasting principle. Ariadne is the last nod to the goddess on Crete; then she is deserted. We may be tempted to ask in her case, why do bad things happen to good people? The epilogue to the myth gives an interesting answer. It seems that Ariadne was destined all along, not for a mortal lover, but an immortal one. The god Dionysius visited the island, fell in love with her and made her his wife, whereupon Zeus raised her to immortality. It is this part of the myth that Strauss focuses on in his dramatic opera, *Ariadne auf Naxos*.

Dionysius was a new form of an old god making his way west from Asia. God of the vine and hence of intoxication and ecstasy, he was also known as the constantly dying and rising god who periodically goes into and comes out of the ocean. Some versions of the myth say that Dionysius had claimed Ariadne as his bride long before Theseus arrived on the scene and that she had betrayed the god turning from a divine to a human lover, and hence was punished by Theseus' abandonment. As god of ecstasy, Dionysius is closely connected with the emotions and the feeling side of life, so he could properly appreciate the feminine. He was said to have a band of women followers. Whether Ariadne consciously or unconsciously betrayed Dionysius, the myth seems to be saying that the tragedy of her abandonment opened the way for her to experience a higher connection with life, to allow the divine to fully enter her life in a way it had not done so before. Abandoned by a mortal who could not fully appreciate her, she found a higher claim in the transcendent, which properly valued her.

It is appropriate that Dionysius is the god who claimed her. As the dying god who represents both divine ecstasy and destructive madness, both life and death, he comes to Ariadne as she is experiencing the sorrow of desertion. Out of her own inner death she moves forward again into a higher life. When united with the divine element, we can move back and forth between joy and sorrow in a new way. Unlike Medea, who chose a destructive path of revenge when abandoned, Ariadne chose a higher way to cope. She grieved and felt fully her sorrow, but was able then to move beyond it instead of wallowing in it. Ariadne points to a higher option in dealing with tragedy.

Perseus and Medusa: Conquest of the Gorgon

Just as Theseus is a more evolved hero than Jason, so we come now to Perseus, who is a more conscious ego than Theseus. Although Perseus is sometimes decried as the slayer of Medusa's feminine power, he can equally be seen as a hero who learns how to absorb the feminine qualities and put them to practical use. He does definitely represent the patriarchal hero who slays the threatening aspect of the feminine, but his coming-of-age story brings him into contact with a new consciousness and clarity of life purpose.

Perseus is another demi-god, son of Zeus and the mortal Danae, daughter of the king of Argos. And his is a most wondrous virgin birth story! It seems that King Acrisius of Argos had been told by the Delphic oracle that his daughter would bear a son who would cause his death. He had his daughter, Danae imprisoned in an underground chamber where no man could see her. Omnipotent Zeus, however, fell in love with the beautiful maiden and appeared to her in a shower of gold. From this visit Perseus was conceived, a true solar hero.

When the enraged king discovered his daughter had given birth to a son, he set them adrift on the sea in a wooden chest. In this way he thought to rid himself of them both without resorting to murder. Inside the chest on a tossing sea, Danae prayed to the gods for help. At last the chest floated to the island of Seriphos. There they were rescued by a kind fisherman named Dictys, who took them into his home and helped to raise Perseus. Eventually King Polydictys of Seriphos noticed Danae and wanted her for his wife, but she refused him because he was a cruel and ruthless man. As Perseus was by now an adolescent and protective of his mother, the king knew he would have to get rid of him first if he intended to force Danae to marry him.

Another crafty politician like Pelias, the king planned a way to send Perseus on an impossible mission, which turned out to be another heroic quest. The king gave a special banquet at which all the male guests were expected to present the host with a horse. Perseus too was invited, although he had nothing to give. When Perseus realized that he was the only one who had no horse to give, he promised to bring Polydictys something else that the king claimed to want - the head of the Gorgon Medusa. Here again we have a youth enthusiastically taking on a dangerous challenge that will prove his worth to the adult world.

Medusa was one of the widely feared Gorgons, three sisters who lived in a foul cavern and were reputed to be so ugly that their very look turned men to stone. Medusa, the only mortal one of the three, was said to have been very beautiful originally. Unfortunately she had incurred the wrath of the virgin goddess Athena by making love in her temple and boasting that she was as beautiful as the goddess. For this indiscretion the goddess turned her wavy ringlets of hair into writhing snakes and her face so ugly that a single glance from it petrified people into stone.

This rivalry between Medusa and Athena may be historical in that there was a goddess of wisdom known in northwest Africa as Medusa. She was part of an ancient triple goddess embodying Wisdom, Strength and Universality. Athena's cruelty to her may have been the Greek way of raising their goddess of wisdom above the African one and emphasizing their superior divinity. It was ironic that the very serpentine aspect of Medusa that made her so ugly was also a statement of her power harking back to the ancient symbol of serpents as the creative power of the feminine, often associated with the Great Goddess. A female face surrounded by serpent hair was an ancient symbol of divine female wisdom. Medusa's punishment graphically expressed patriarchal fear of the ancient goddess power. The Hebrew tale of Adam and Eve and the serpent in the Garden of Eden is another patriarchal attempt to downgrade the feminine serpent power by blaming original sin on it. Conversely in India the Kudalini life force is described as the serpent power, and the revered goddess Kali is pictured with serpents entwined around her. Kali represents the dark and devouring aspect of the feminine, as Medusa represents the dark and cruel aspect of Athena.

So Perseus' quest of self-assertion is to encounter the dark devouring side of the feminine and conquer it. Perhaps this is appropriate for a youth who had known only a mother and not a father and needed to move out of the shadow of the maternal. Just as a child's self-assertion as an adult releases him from the narrowness of the role as son, so does it also release the mother from the narrowness of her role as parent. His success on this quest will bring release not only for himself, but also for his mother and the forced marriage from which he must protect her. The whole quest is therefore an encounter with the feminine, and Perseus goes about it in an interior way.

As soon as he had taken on the challenge of her enemy Medusa, Athena was interested and brought her higher wisdom to aid him. She told him that he would need three items in this quest—a helmet to make him invisible, winged shoes to fly over Medusa, and a wallet to carry back the decapitated head. These special items all representing inner power could only be obtained from the Nymphs of the North, three beautiful sisters who dwelt on a mountain (raised consciousness) and guarded life-giving fountains. But first he must seek out the Graea, three ancient sisters in the underworld who shared a single eye. They alone could tell him where to find the elusive Nymphs of the North. However he would first have to find a way to get them to divulge this secret.

Athena next gave him a shield of polished brass so that he could look indirectly upon Medusa's mirror image in the shield and not be affected by her petrifying glance. She also brought to him Hermes, the messenger of the gods, who can be a guide from one level of awareness to another. Hermes gave him a curved sword to fit Medusa's neck and then led Perseus to the Graea in the underworld. It is interesting to note that Perseus must deal here with three sets of three sisters each, another form of the triple goddess or the feminine. Going to the ancient wisdom of the Graea in the underworld represents a descent into the unconscious with its unitary eye of holistic perception before conscious differentiation. This is an appropriate first step in a quest of the feminine.

When Perseus saw the three old women sitting in a circle passing their single eye of perception around, he realized how to get the secret of the Nymphs from them. Tuning into their rhythm in passing the eye and noting how it went around the circle, he anticipated when and where it would be passed and grabbed it during one of those times. Now that he had gained their unified perception, they had no choice but to tell him what he wanted in order to get their eye back. Grumbling, they gave the secret directions to the Nymphs of the North. Such attuning to the rhythm of the unconscious is the first step in encountering the higher consciousness of the Nymphs.

Leaving the underworld and climbing up the mountain, Perseus next sought out the higher awareness of the Nymphs of the North, guardians of the life-giving fountains, the upwelling source of renewal. The Nymphs were joyful and generous, emotionally sustained by their fountains. They gladly gave the power to approach the Gorgons. All of their gifts suggest that this was really an interior journey. The invisible helmet suggests the power to travel in imagination, unseen by the outside world. The winged shoes give the ability to rise above the challenge and not get stuck in a devouring situation. The wallet to enclose Medusa's head would keep him from being petrified by her power. It would provide the objectivity which enabled him to carry her with him without losing his own initiative.

With these gifts of higher consciousness, together with Athena's shield for a non-directive approach and Hermes' sword curved to fit the situation, Perseus was now ready to approach his adversary. Once again he took time and tuned into the Gorgons, searching for Medusa in the shield. Being well prepared by the higher wisdom of Athena and his own growing perception of the feminine, he had no trouble then zooming in on her in his invisible helmet and winged shoes and achieving his purpose. Immediately he put the severed head in the wallet and flew upward.

To his great amazement, from Medusa's drops of blood falling into the sea, there sprang up the winged horse Pegasus. Pegasus later had adventures with other heroes, but he is usually associated with poetry because he later becomes the property of the Muses. In the myth of Medusa he represents the creative power that can spring up when the deadening mask of judgment has been removed. He is the new life conceived in the Temple of Athena and never allowed to be born while the stone facade was kept in place. Perseus, with the aid of higher wisdom, overcomes the devouring aspect of the feminine and allows the creative impulse to spring forth.

But that is not the end of the story. On his way back to Seriphos, Perseus spotted a beautiful young maiden chained to a hillside, waiting to be devoured by a dreadful sea monster. Alighting beside her, he asked her why she was in this tragic situation and discovered that Andromeda was the victim of her mother's foolish boast that she was more beautiful than the sea nymphs. Such overweening pride brought retribution from the Sea God, Poseidon, who sent a sea monster to lay waste her husband's kingdom. Andromeda's father, the king, had to promise to sacrifice his daughter to save his kingdom.

Perseus immediately offered to unbind her, but she nobly refused, saying that the welfare of the kingdom depended on her sacrifice. This is a typical response of the unliberated feminine power, which may be too willing to sacrifice itself for others. Perseus then told her parents that he would slay the sea monster if he could have Andromeda as his bride. Using the gifts he had acquired—the invisible helmet, the winged sandals and the sword of Hermes, he rose above the monster. Protected by his helmet of invisibility, he overcame the beast before it could get to Andromeda. Having learned the process for himself, he was now able to save Andromeda from her devouring mother's narcissism that would have cut off the young maiden's potential. Andromeda needed to encounter the masculine polarity to achieve her liberation, just as Perseus had needed to encounter the feminine for his.

While they were all celebrating at the betrothal banquet, a complication ensued when Andromeda's former fiancé arrived with his warriors to claim his bride. It seems the parents had neglected to mention this prior engagement to Perseus. Andromeda was horrified by this interruption. She realized that her new champion was much nobler than the old one. Her former fiancé had not undergone a maturing quest and had instead cowardly left her to face the sea monster alone. Perseus fought bravely against the intruders, but was outnumbered. At last he thought of his secret weapon, the

Gorgon's head. Holding it aloft, he turned his adversaries to stone and won back his bride. Together they returned to Seriphos. There Perseus discovered that King Polydictes had imprisoned his mother Danae for refusing to marry him. The king was surprised to see him and laughed when Perseus announced that he had possession of Medusa's head. In reply Perseus opened the wallet and showed him the head, thereby turning him to stone. The people urged Perseus to become their king, but he graciously refused and made his benefactor, the humble fisherman Dictys, king instead. Then he took his wife and mother back to his rightful land of Argos.

His grandfather Acrisius was away on business, so Perseus decided to participate in the athletic games being held in a kingdom to the north. There he hurled a discus which struck and killed an aged spectator, who turned out to be none other than Acrisius. And so the oracle was fulfilled whereby he caused his grandfather's death. No one blamed him for the accident, though, and he succeeded to the throne of Argos. The new hero, matured through his quest, now replaces the old king as ruler.

Perseus ruled wisely and well, later founding the kingdom of Mycenae known as the center of a thriving golden civilization. Perseus and Andromeda had a son, Perses from whom the Persian kings later claimed descent. Eventually Perseus gave the Gorgon's head to Athena, who placed it in the middle of her shield for protection. Whenever Athena flashed her shield with its stone-faced judgmental aspect, she could be sure people would keep their distance.

The story of Perseus and Andromeda brought out the Pegasus of creativity in the American sculptor, Daniel Chester French, who carved the Lincoln Memorial. The very last work he sculpted before his death in 1931 was a statue of Andromeda chained to the rock. He felt she represented the imprisonment of women in society, and her eminent release was a symbol of the coming age of emancipation for women that had begun with the Suffrage Movement in the United States. Pegasus has prompted a number of twentieth century writers to find inspiration in mythology.

The story of Perseus and his encounter with the feminine need not be construed as a patriarchal disempowering of Medusa, even if that was part of the impetus for the story. On its deeper level, it traces a universal journey to a higher appreciation of feminine wisdom. Perseus, in the quest for his own identity, goes from victim to victor, working with the feminine wisdom to develop imagination, to learn how to attune to his adversary, to rise above the challenge of the devouring feminine, to release creative inspiration, and to gain new consciousness. This enables him to release his mother and his female partner from their imprisonment and to establish a marriage of nobility, eventually begetting a golden civilization. The solar hero or developing ego encounters the feminine and is not destroyed by its threatening aspect, but rises to a new level of consciousness, aided by the higher feminine wisdom.

Psyche and Eros: Soul and Spirit

The story of Psyche and Eros is a latecomer to Greek mythology. It comes to us in written form by way of Lucius Apuleius in the second century C.E. As noted earlier, Apuleius' novel, *The Golden Ass* is understood to be a disguised account of an initiation into the Mysteries of Isis. The myth of Psyche and Eros, refined from an old Greek folktale, is told as a story within a story. In *The Golden Ass* a young woman is kidnapped on her wedding day, and an old woman set to watch over her tells the myth to comfort her. The old woman seems to be a symbol for Hecate, the wise old crone, bringing wisdom about the maturing of the feminine principle to the young bride.

For here we have a myth about the initiation of a heroine in which the untried feminine energy is challenged by the masculine and becomes more aware. In the preceding myths of mortals, the hero or Yang energy interacts with the feminine to develop a mature ego. The classic quest of the hero is that of finding outer power. It has to do with one's career and one's actions in the outer world. The quest of the heroine or Yin energy is that of finding inner power and becoming conscious of one's capacity to love.

Psyche is the Greek name for butterfly, the creature that transforms from a lowly caterpillar into the luminous beauty of a butterfly able to rise above the world and spread its beauty. Psyche was sometimes represented in art as a maiden with the wings of a butterfly. Psyche also means soul in Greek, pointing to the transformational capacity of our being.

Erich Neumann, in his remarkable analysis of this myth, *Amor and Psyche*, views Psyche as a new and higher form of Aphrodite coming into human consciousness. She is a transformation of the primitive love goddess into a more evolved one. Robert Johnson also emphasizes this evolution in his popular study, *She*, exploring the feminine pattern of individuation from a Jungian viewpoint.

Aphrodite is the real protagonist of the story, and she becomes a catalyst for Psyche's growth throughout the myth. When Aphrodite became aware that people were paying more attention to a beautiful young princess named Psyche than they were to the Goddess of Love, her jealousy was stirred. We are told that the Princess Psyche, youngest daughter of a king and queen, was not only more beautiful than Aphrodite, but she was so kind and gracious that people almost literally worshipped her and were already calling her the "new Aphrodite." Naturally this was very threatening to the Goddess, for her temple was empty and she was being replaced in the human mind by another. Her more physical, sensual beauty was being challenged by one who had beauty of spirit as well as form. And the primitive instinct of the old archetype of beauty was enraged. She would punish this rival and show her who was more powerful!

Aphrodite determined that the best punishment for Psyche would be to have eligible men avoid her and have Psyche fall in love with an ugly, vile person who would bring her unhappiness. First she put a curse on Psyche that no suitor would approach her. Then she bid her son Eros take his arrows of love and two bottles of love potion, one of passion and one of bittersweet essence. When the young Eros flew off to pour them on his mother's rival, he was so startled by Psyche's beauty that he dropped the bottle of passion and spilled it on himself. Falling in love with Psyche on the spot, he decided not to pour the bittersweet one on her.

In this act of disobedience to his mother, Eros too was starting to come of age. He journeys away from the power of the mother to find his own feminine in Psyche. But in the beginning he merely goes back to Mother, whining that he finds Psyche too beautiful for the bittersweet potion.

Disgusted by her son, Aphrodite had to take other measures. While she pondered this, her curse was preventing suitable men from marrying Psyche. Her two older sisters found husbands, but no one approached Psyche. All the men would worship and flatter her, but no one would ask for her hand in marriage, thinking her above them. Psyche became a lonely object of adoration, with no true companionship. Her parents finally consulted an oracle to see what the problem was, thinking they must have unwittingly incurred the wrath of the gods. The oracle, influenced by Aphrodite, replied that Psyche was not destined for a mortal lover. Her future husband was a monster, who was awaiting her at the top of a mountain. Now a royal family always had to heed an oracle, for fear of what would happen to their kingdom. Sorrowfully the parents dressed her in bridal finery and led her to the top of the mountain, leaving her there alone to meet her fate.

In folklore the mountaintop is usually symbolically associated with higher consciousness or going up to a new level of understanding. Perseus, you will remember, climbed the mountain in order to receive the higher gifts of the Nymphs of the North. As Psyche awaited her doom alone on the mountaintop, a gentle wind sent by Eros came and wafted her away to a lovely meadow with flowers, fountains and a golden palace appearing out of nowhere. Again Eros has defied his mother and thwarted her plans, in the pursuit of his own love interest. A voice commanded Psyche to enter the palace, where a magnificent feast had been laid out for her. Heavenly music was heard for her entertainment, and she was instructed to enjoy herself before retiring to the bedroom to await her husband.

When it was dark, a form appeared in the bedroom and gently made love to her without revealing his identity. He spent the night with her, but left before the light of dawn. Psyche's life took on a predictable, if mystifying pattern with days of enjoying the delights of the palace and gardens and beautiful nights of love with her unknown husband, who always left before morning. She begged to see him and know who he was, but he told her only that she must ask no questions of him and must not see him during the day. Had he not provided her with many delights in his absence? This has a familiar ring to it. Some men today also choose to keep their wives or lovers in the dark without revealing their true selves or emotions. They may shut their partners out of their daytime life and relate to them only on the sexual level. It is the complaint of numerous women of our time, no matter how well provided for they may be.

But all the delights of the palace and gardens began to pall, for Psyche felt like a prisoner at the mercy of an unknown force. Being also lonely, she asked to have her two older sisters visit her. Her husband opposed this knowing they would ask questions of her which he did not want raised. She wept and begged so much, though, that he eventually reluctantly agreed.

The next day she met her two sisters in the meadow and joyfully showed them her palace and grounds. They were quite surprised, for they had supposed her dead. Naturally curious about her mysterious husband, they plied her with questions about him. Unable to answer their questions, Psyche stammered excuses and tried to change the subject. Her confusion was evident, though, for she would describe him in one way and then later picture him differently. Envious at her good fortune, for they had always been jealous of her outstanding beauty that made them feel ordinary by comparison, the sisters filled her mind with suspicion that her husband must be a monster, just as the oracle had prophesied.

In succeeding visits when she had to admit that he would tell her nothing about himself, they instructed her to wait until he was asleep and then shine a lamp upon him and be prepared to kill the monster with a knife. At first Psyche would not hear of it, for she had a blind loyalty to her unknown husband. Eventually, though, she succumbed to their repeated suspicions and decided to act. Probably only a very naive and trusting soul would have waited so long to investigate the situation.

One evening she hid a lamp and a knife in the bedroom. When Eros had fallen asleep, she carefully lit the lamp and held it over him, wondering what she would see. His youthful beauty so dazzled and shocked her that the lamp shook in her hand and a drop of hot oil from it fell upon Eros. Awakening to find her looking at him with love, but with a knife in her hand, he knew at once that the sisters had pushed her to this act. Unable to relate to her in the full glare of consciousness and unwilling to confront his mother's rage, he told her sadly that he must leave her forever.

Immediately the palace and gardens disappeared, and Psyche found herself back home. There she told her sisters what had happened. Each of them was unhappily married and secretly felt that now Eros would surely choose her since Psyche was out of the picture. Each of them climbed the mountain and leaned into the wind. With such impure and selfish motivation, of course, they were not ready for higher consciousness and fell from the cliff to their deaths. Psyche, having now asserted herself, could not really go home again to her parents for she was beyond that. When she first met Eros blindly, she had the love that she needed for completion and so had a kind of paradise for a while. But that paradise came at a high price. Eros' demand is part of the patriarchal wish that his wife not ask for consciousness, that she be in the dark and obey him, asking no questions and letting him go his own way. But this situation was not conducive to Psyche's growth, and her unmet needs demanded more conscious knowledge. The sisters are that nagging need within that caused Psyche to become conscious of what was lacking in paradise. They are actually the demand for evolution that we all experience in various ways. They are the forces that push us out of self-satisfaction, out of our naive paradise, into new discoveries about our true situation. Whatever the motivation, they demand that we stop hiding from reality. There is often a high cost when we decide to do that, for we are overturning the old order.

Psyche had decided to assert herself and really look at the relationship. She needed to see her lover as he really was. In Jungian terms she is looking at her own animus or masculine energy so that she is no longer dominated by it. So she provided herself with the lamp of clarity for full consciousness and the knife for discrimination. She was going to illuminate the situation and cut out the control.

When she saw Eros in this way, she truly fell in love with him. But the punishment for consciousness was loss of paradise and his absence. Eros, who had wanted to keep her in the dark and control the relationship, now went home to Mother. He was not mature enough for a conscious relationship. Mother unsympathetically reminded him that she knew that woman was trouble and was secretly glad to have her son back all to herself.

Psyche, though, was faithful to her love and sought out the other goddesses for advice on returning to him. All the goddesses were fearful of Aphrodite's vindictiveness and told her she must go to Aphrodite herself. Her first reaction was despair, and she threw herself into the river, wanting to drown in her emotions. The river threw her back up, and she encountered Pan on the riverbank. Pan was an archaic pastoral god, from whom we get the word "panic." He was an appropriate god to meet, for she was truly in panic. He told her she must seek out Eros and be reunited with love. In the midst of her panic, a clear mandate emerged. To regain Eros, she must first confront her rival Aphrodite.

In fear and trembling Psyche went to visit her disdainful mother-in-law. Aphrodite sent her handmaidens Habit and Trouble to greet her, refusing to see her immediately. They typically made her uncomfortable for a while and finally took her in humiliation to the goddess to beg a reunion with her son. Aphrodite now had the upper hand and set for Psyche, not one, but four impossible tasks to accomplish. Since the heroes had traditionally one challenge to overcome, could this be a subtle suggestion that it takes four times as much energy and patience to develop the Yin energy as the Yang?

Although Aphrodite appears to persecute Psyche, in actuality the four tasks she sets prove to be stages of evolution for her inner development. As such, Aphrodite is the catalyst for the emergence of a new element in Psyche, pushing her to growth. Jean Bolen gives an excellent description of these tasks in her chapter on Aphrodite in *Goddesses in Everywoman*. Robert Johnson does likewise in *She* and both should be consulted for in-depth discussion. Their ideas will be only summarized here briefly. For her first task Psyche had to sort within one day a huge roomful of seeds, separating them into groups of individual grains. The real task in psychological terms is the necessary process of sorting through our conflicting feelings and values to see each one for what it is and separate out our priorities. This can seem overwhelming when our emotions are all jumbled up, as in the room of seeds, but it can be done with the right help.

Eros finally started to take responsibility for his reunion with Psyche when he saw her faithfulness to him. He watched her trials from afar and stirred up an ant hill which marched into the room and accomplished the sorting within the day. Ants are by nature well organized for this task. They represent that natural sorting process we all possess but need to learn to call upon when feelings and priorities are in confusion. They are the potential Yang energy that can make order out of confusion.

The second task imposed on Psyche was to obtain some of the golden fleece from the rams of the sun, ferocious beasts that could easily destroy her. The challenge here is to acquire power without being destroyed by it. Psyche's way of obtaining the golden fleece was very different from Jason's. As she gazed at the powerful beasts across the river, the rustling reeds in the river told her to wait and observe the rams. At the height of the sun they would gather by the bushes for shelter from its glare, and later in the day when they left the meadow, she could safely pick clumps of their fleece left on the bushes. The flexible reeds were telling her to wait patiently for power and gather it indirectly without a confrontational power play that could destroy her. The feminine way is to gather power in appropriate amounts and in a way that allows for compassionate assimilation rather than gaining it by overpowering another. This Psyche did and obtained her golden fleece.

Her third task now was to fill a crystal goblet with water from the highest spring in the world which streamed down and eventually fed the River Styx of the Underworld. Flowing from the highest spring to the lowest depth underground, the water represents the circular flow of life into which she must drop. Psyche started climbing up to the spring, but soon saw that it was out of her reach because of the sheer cliffs surrounding it. At this point an eagle came to her aid. Grasping the goblet in its beak, he swooped over the spring and dipped into it, filling the container.

The eagle represents the ability to see the whole panorama of life from a higher perspective. By maintaining an objective overview, we can then focus on one significant spot and grasp its importance for us. The total life force could run over us and drown us if we could not choose a small part of it to carry in our individual ego. Psyche was learning to develop the eagle's eye objective view of life and focus on the creative task appropriate to her.

Her final task was to take an empty box to Persephone in the Underworld and ask for some of her beauty ointment for Aphrodite. Not knowing how to get to the Underworld except through death, Psyche intended to throw herself off a tower into the arms of death. Before she could jump, however, the tower came to her aid and told her a better way to get to the Underworld. Built by human intellect and effort, the tower represents that ability within us to look at a situation with the intellect and find a better way. She was to take coins for the ferryman at the River Styx and bread for the three-headed dog Cerberus who guarded the entrance. Most importantly she was to refuse to give help to any who begged of her on the way. This is a startling requirement, for frequently the test in folkloric initiations is to see if the initiate is willing to help another. When the hero is male, usually the need is to develop compassion. However, this is one of the worst traps for many women who tend to place the needs of others above their own and become diverted from their own goals. Had Psyche been a selfish person to begin with, the requirement might have been different. But for her, as for many women, the harder challenge is to harden her heart and learn to say no to the infinitesimal needs of' others in order to listen to her own heart. None of us can determine our life course until we can say no to the things that distract us. We do not need to do others' work for them, no matter how compassionate we may be. Each of us must do our own inner work.

Three times Psyche had pathetic persons begging her for help, but each time she was able to focus on her own mission and not be distracted from it. In the Underworld Persephone was gracious and gladly filled the box with her beauty ointment. The only condition was that Psyche must not open the box before giving it to Aphrodite. This is the one condition Psyche could not meet. If Aphrodite, Goddess of Beauty herself, needed something of Persephone's beauty, Psyche knew it must be very special indeed.

What Persephone possessed, of course, was a spiritual beauty that only death of the ego and rebirth could bring. Psyche was unconsciously hungering for this, although she did not know what it was. She only knew that it must be very special and she yearned to discover it. And so, when she had safely returned from the underworld, which had activated this desire, she opened the box.

The moment she did this, a deep sleep came upon her, for Persephone's beauty is the spiritual experience of psychological death, of transformation from one level of development to another. The old consciousness of her concern for physical beauty had to die to a new consciousness of spiritual beauty. This beauty was born from the developmental tasks she had undertaken, which brought a new maturity and sense of self. So Psyche did experience a death and rebirth that had nothing to do with losing her life.

The rebirth occurred when Eros then came to her directly to revive her and to claim her as his own. For just as Psyche had become more autonomous through all her trials, Eros also had been growing away from his mother and now was able to assert himself for his beloved in the face of his mother's opposition. Psyche had done her inner work and fulfilled the conditions of a reunion with Eros. Her patient and loving loyalty had helped him to understand the depth of her love, and he was now willing to speak up for her and honor her. He claimed her as his bride and went to great Zeus himself to ask that she be admitted to Olympus and recognized as divinity also. Agreeing that she deserved it, Zeus exalted her to divine status.

Thus honored by Eros, the masculine principle, Psyche gave birth to a daughter named Joy. Joy always comes when we actualize our potential. Joseph Campbell calls it "following our bliss". Aphrodite grudgingly accepted the inevitable, for she too had seen a new face of love and knew that Psyche represented the new archetype of spiritual beauty wedded to physical love, Eros. Both of them are her children and represent the next generation, the next step for humanity.

The myth is sometimes interpreted as an allegory of the human soul being purified by suffering and misfortune as preparation for true happiness and love. This is a somewhat moralistic view that seems too facile and a bit righteous. It is more useful to see it as a metaphor of the vulnerable soul gaining skills and developing animus energy to rise to a new level of consciousness that unites Yin and Yang energy for a transformation.

This is actually a coming-of-age for both Psyche and Eros. Each stimulated the other to move to a higher level of consciousness that neither one could have done without the other. Dare we to believe that such an evolution of the masculine and the feminine, such a uniting of right and left brain, of balancing Yin and Yang could lead to a higher, more joyous humanity?

Epilogue

Ancient mythology has indeed given us colorful characters in which to see ourselves mirrored. We can probably see a bit of each of the gods and goddesses, heroes and heroines in ourselves. But just as ancient divinities amalgamate several archetypes into one or conversely subdivide an original archetype into lesser ones, so our understanding of life continues to change and evolve. Isis became an amalgam of various fertility goddesses in the ancient world, but was split into Hera, Demeter, Persephone and Aphrodite in the Greek world. Different cultures and periods of history will choose how they deal with these archetypes. Psyche points us to a higher form of Aphrodite. Perseus is a more evolved hero than Theseus, who in turn is more advanced than Jason.

The potential for change and higher growth lies in us all. Change is not easy. Nor is it always as dramatic as the myths. Their drama merely points out a possibility. Each of us is privileged to create our own myth and to live the drama of our own life. May these ancient myths revitalize the inner journey we each experience. For this is how society as a whole is enriched.

The gods and goddesses are very much alive in our time. They are us. And we can create our own Olympus.

Acknowledgements

I wish to acknowledge my gratitude to: Jean Bolyn, whose books and workshops provided the impetus for this book; Elaine Stuart and James Scherer for expert guidance in dream work; Kimberly Burnham, whose vision and computer expertise made this book a reality; Pat Caffrey for a final nudge to publish in print; Linda Scacco for critiquing the manuscript; Della Hennelly and Sherry Williams for encouragement; And finally, all the participants in my Mythology classes sponsored by the Adult Education Program of West Hartford, CT. Their enthusiasm provided much joy on this journey.

Suggested Reading and Additional Resources

1. Bolen, Jean. *Goddesses in Everywoman: A New Psychology of Women*. San Francisco: Harper & Row, 1984.

2. Campbell, Joseph. *The Hero With a Thousand Faces*. Princeton: Princeton University Press, 1968.

3. Campbell, Joseph. *The Power of Myth*. New York: Doubleday, 1988.

4. Eliade, Mircea. *Rites and Symbols of Initiation*. New York: Harper & Row, 1958.

5. French, Marilyn. *Beyond Power: Men, Women and Morals*. New York: Summit Books, 1985.

6. Gimbutas, Marija. *The Language of the Goddess*. London: Thames and Hudson, 1989.

7. Grant, Michael and Hazel, John. *Gods and Mortals in Classical Mythology*. Springfield, Massachusetts, G. & C. Merriam Company, 1973.

8. Graves, Robert. *The Greek Myths*. New York: Penguin Books, 1960.

9. Graves, Robert. *The White Goddess*. New York: Creative Age Press, 1948.

10. Hamilton, Edith. *Mythology*. Boston: Little, Brown &Company, 1942.

11. Jacobi, Jolande. *The Way of Individuation*. New York: Harcourt, Brace, 1967.

12. Johnson, Robert. *She: Understanding Feminine Psychology*. New York: Harper & Row, 1977.

13. Jung, Carl. *Man and His Symbols*. Garden City: Doubleday, 1964.

14. Jung, Emma. *Animus and Anima*. Dallas: Spring Publications, 1957.

15. Knight, Gareth. *The Rose Cross and the Goddess: The Quest for the Eternal Feminine Principle*. New York: Destiny Books, 1985.

16. Miller, William. *Your Golden Shadow: Discovering and Fulfilling Your Undeveloped Self*. San Francisco: Harper &Row, 1989.

17. Neumann, Erich. *Amor and Psyche: The Psychic Development of the Feminine* Bollingen Series LIV. Princeton: Princeton University Press, 1971.

18. Whitmont, Edward C. *Return of the Goddess*. New York: Crossroad, 1982.

Index

Adonis, 26, 53, 54, 55, 56
Aphrodite, 3, 8, 18, 19, 22, 26, 31, 48, 49, 50, 51, 52, 53, 54, 55, 56, 61, 65, 71, 76, 91, 92, 97, 100, 101, 102, 104
Apollo, 3, 11, 17, 21, 40, 41, 42, 43, 44, 45, 46, 47
Ares, 18, 50, 51, 52, 54, 61
Ariadne, 3, 5, 8, 9, 69, 72, 73, 75, 76, 77, 78, 79
Artemis, 3, 7, 8, 11, 17, 21, 22, 39, 40, 41, 42, 43, 44, 45, 46, 47, 55
Eros, 3, 5, 8, 31, 50, 56, 90, 92, 93, 95, 96, 97, 98, 102, 103
Hades, 3, 8, 32, 33, 34, 35, 37, 38
Hera, 3, 5, 7, 8, 12, 13, 16, 17, 18, 19, 20, 21, 22, 23, 24, 25, 26, 30, 31, 34, 40, 41, 43, 53, 59, 60, 61, 67, 104
Isis, 3, 5, 10, 13, 26, 27, 28, 29, 30, 31, 32, 34, 36, 90, 104
Jason, 3, 5, 8, 12, 21, 55, 57, 59, 60, 61, 62, 63, 64, 65, 66, 67, 77, 80, 99, 104

Medea, 3, 5, 8, 11, 12, 55, 57, 61, 62, 63, 64, 65, 66, 67, 68, 69, 70, 79
Medusa, 3, 9, 80, 81, 82, 83, 84, 85, 87, 88
Osiris, 3, 5, 10, 13, 26, 27, 28, 29, 36, 54
Persephone, 3, 8, 17, 26, 27, 32, 33, 34, 35, 36, 37, 38, 39, 42, 53, 54, 74, 100, 101, 104
Perseus, 3, 5, 9, 17, 80, 81, 82, 83, 84, 85, 86, 87, 88, 93, 104
Psyche, 3, 5, 8, 9, 31, 32, 37, 50, 55, 56, 90, 91, 92, 93, 94, 95, 96, 97, 98, 99, 100, 101, 102, 103, 104, 107
Theseus, 3, 5, 8, 9, 55, 60, 65, 69, 70, 71, 72, 73, 74, 75, 76, 77, 78, 80, 104
Yang, 13, 14, 15, 18, 20, 23, 24, 40, 45, 50, 77, 90, 97, 98, 103
Yin, 13, 14, 15, 18, 20, 21, 23, 24, 31, 39, 40, 45, 50, 68, 90, 97, 103
Zeus, 3, 5, 7, 8, 12, 13, 16, 17, 18, 19, 20, 21, 22, 23, 24, 25, 32, 33, 35, 37, 40, 49, 50, 52, 54, 59, 78, 80, 102